PENGUIN LIFE

# WHEN THINGS DON'T GO YOUR WAY

Haemin Sunim is a Korean Zen Buddhist teacher and author of two bestselling books, *The Things You Can See Only When You Slow Down* and *Love for Imperfect Things*. His books have sold over 6 million copies worldwide and have been translated into thirty-eight languages. Born in South Korea, he came to the United States to study film, only to find himself pulled into the spiritual life. Educated at UC Berkeley, Harvard, and Princeton, he received formal monastic training in Korea and taught at Hampshire College in Amherst, Massachusetts, for seven years. His books are popular as guides not only to meditation but also to overcoming the challenges of modern life. When not traveling to share his teachings, Sunim lives in Seoul, where he founded Dharma Illumination Zen Center, which offers meditation retreats and counseling programs.

# When Things Don't Go Your Way

*Zen Wisdom for Difficult Times*

Haemin Sunim

*Translated by*
Charles La Shure and Haemin Sunim

life

PENGUIN BOOKS
An imprint of Penguin Random House LLC
penguinrandomhouse.com



Portions of this book were originally published in Korean as 고요할수록 밝아지는 것들 (*Goyohalsurok Balgajineun ggeokdeul*) by 수오서재 (Suoseojae), Paju, South Korea.

A Penguin Life Book

LIBRARY OF CONGRESS CATALOGING-IN-PUBLICATION DATA
Names: Hyemin, author, translator. | La Shure, Charles, translator.
Title: When things don't go your way : Zen wisdom for difficult times / Haemin Sunim; translated by Charles La Shure and Haemin Sunim.
Description: New York City: Penguin, 2024. | The unverified Korean title is: Tangsin i purhaeng hal ttae kiŏk haeya hal mal. | Translated from Korean.
Identifiers: LCCN 2023025995 (print) | LCCN 2023025996 (ebook) | ISBN 9780143135890 (hardcover) | ISBN 9780525507475 (ebook)
Subjects: LCSH: Suffering—Religious aspects—Buddhism. | Resilience (Personality trait)—Religious aspects—Buddhism. | Zen Buddhism—Doctrines. | Spiritual life—Zen Buddhism.
Classification: LCC BQ4235 .H9413 2024 (print) | LCC BQ4235 (ebook) | DDC 294.3/4442—dc23/eng/20230921
LC record available at https://lccn.loc.gov/2023025995
LC ebook record available at https://lccn.loc.gov/2023025996

Printed in the United States of America
2nd Printing

Set in Centaur MT Pro

Quotes noted as * have been attributed to the speaker listed.

# Contents

Introduction vii

Chapter 1:
When Things Don't Go Your Way

Don't Be All Right 2
Why Are We Unhappy? 19
How Do You Feel About the Universe? 37

Chapter 2:
When Your Heart Is Aching

Please Reject Me Gently! 44
Spring Days Are Gone 63
My Jealousy, My Suffering 82

## Chapter 3:
## When Feeling Burned Out and Joyless

Small but Certain Happiness 88
Where Is Your *Querencia*? 104
Finding Peace in a Restless Mind 120

## Chapter 4:
## When Loneliness Visits

Why Are We Lonely? 126
A New Era of "Alone Together" 141
Seeing Loneliness as It Is 155

## Chapter 5:
## When Facing Uncertainty

The Courage to Say "I Can't" 160
The Two Me's Inside of Me 175
Listen First to the Pain Inside of You 193

## Chapter 6:
## When Enlightenment Has Yet to Occur

Ways of Living Harmoniously 198
Discovering Your True Self 213
The Tale of Roundy's Great Journey 225

# Introduction

A LONELY, MIDDLE-AGED MAN LIVED by himself in a small village. One day, he heard a knock at his door and found an incredibly graceful lady standing there, dressed in heavenly clothes and adorned with stunning jewels. Enchanted by her beauty and delightful scent, the man kindly asked her who she was. She replied, "I am the Goddess of Pleasant Virtue. I have come to bestow upon you great prosperity, success, and love." Overjoyed at her words, the man immediately invited her in and prepared a feast in her honor.

A short time later, the man heard another knock at his door. Upon answering, he saw a woman dressed in tattered clothing, with a terrible odor. The man asked her why she was at his door. She replied, "I am the Goddess of Unpleasant Darkness. I have come to bring poverty, failure, and loneliness into your life." Fearful of her words, the man asked her to leave immediately. However, she then stated, "I follow wherever my twin sister goes. If you want my sister to stay, you must also invite me in." When he asked the Goddess of Pleasant Virtue if this was true, she nodded her head and said, "We are a pair. You cannot accept one without the other."

This tale from the Nirvana Sutra illustrates how good fortune often leads to unforeseen disappointments and hardships. Although we desire only positive experiences in life, it is inevitable that we will also encounter difficult times. These challenges, however, are not without purpose. They can serve as valuable opportunities for self-discovery that can lead to emotional maturity and spiritual growth. The extent of the maturity and growth often corresponds to the severity of the situation we face. We learn to be patient, courageous, compassionate, and truthful through the pain we go through.

THIS BOOK DRAWS ON MY personal journey through various struggles and challenges that led to a deep reflection and appreciation of my life, both as a Zen teacher and as a human being. Each of the six chapters features an emotionally challenging time, and consists of three personal essays filled with my stories and advice. Alongside these essays, you will find a collection of short, insightful stanzas that capture either my "a-ha" moments or "ouch" experiences. I hope these reflections provide comfort, hope, and encouragement to those facing difficulties in life. May your journey be blessed with love and kindness as well as many moments of small enlightenment!

# When Things Don't Go Your Way

Chapter 1

# When Things Don’t Go Your Way

# Don't Be All Right

Can you sit still with difficult emotions? Rather than trying to quickly escape from them, are you able to allow them to stay with you and witness how they unfold in your mind?

I know that this goes against our instincts to avoid uncomfortable feelings by any means possible. But for a minute or two, I encourage you to go against your instincts, and let those difficult feelings flow in the space of your mind. For instance, be curious about what would happen if you were to allow a sense of disappointment, sadness, or hurt to linger. Instead of judging yourself for having such feelings, or trying to divert your attention by watching a TV show or surfing the Internet, what if you face them directly and observe unpleasant feelings without any prejudice or resistance?

For a long time, the most difficult emotion for me was the fear of abandonment. Whenever someone canceled a dinner appointment at the last minute, leaving me alone for the evening unexpectedly, or if I didn't hear back within twenty-four hours after sending a text message to a friend, a fear of abandonment was triggered in me. I felt the pain of loneliness and anxiety, as if I had been left out in a field to fend for myself. I frequently thought about worst-case scenarios, including people leaving me without any warning. When triggered, I could also sense a dark existential void, as if it were going to engulf me. I would then seek a way to avoid these uncomfortable feelings while desperately looking for safety and connection.

I feel a little vulnerable sharing this because I am a middle-aged man who also happens to be a Zen teacher. But, like those of many spiritual teachers in the past, my journey also began because of very personal psychological sufferings. Even after sitting on a meditation cushion for many years, it was a mystery to me why I had this fear of abandonment when I had a stable upbringing by loving parents who actually like each other. After the success of my books gained me recognition in South Korea, my fear of abandonment, unfortunately, grew. I was afraid that people might turn their backs on me one day and abandon me for good because of what I said or did.

And then, to my surprise, it actually happened.

In the winter of 2020, I agreed to appear on a Korean TV program that documented the daily life of well-known people. As usual, I started my day with a morning meditation and prayer in the small home where I have been living with my elderly parents for the last five years. I had bought the house for my parents with the royalties from my books and then transferred the ownership to my Buddhist order. However, after the program aired, a small group of people criticized me for not practicing the monastic ideal of "non-possession," without understanding the true reality of a monk's life in Korea: we have no pension or guaranteed housing. Most of us have to fend for ourselves.

Some people started spreading rumors online that this house was opulent and claimed that I possessed a Ferrari. This was frustrating because the house was modest by any measure, and I had never even owned a Korean driving license. To add to all of this, a senior monk, who was also a well-known author in Korea, critiqued me in a series of Facebook posts, denouncing me as a "parasite" and an "entertainer" with no knowledge of "true" Buddhism. For several days after, all the major Korean news outlets made his posts one of their top stories, seemingly eager for me to argue with him in public and generate even more sensational coverage. As I didn't react, countless people online came out and denounced me just like the senior monk had done.

Life had given me many lemons before. But this time, I was given too many lemons to make into lemonade. I was shocked, overwhelmed and deeply hurt. My worst nightmare was coming true. I felt betrayed by my monastic brother and deserted by the people who had previously liked my work. Ironically, I, the founder of the School of Broken Hearts, found myself in urgent need of healing.

When I was new to spiritual practices, I had naively imagined the path as one of moral perfection where practitioners had to eliminate all negative emotions such as anger, hatred, fear, and attachment. As a result, I unconsciously repressed those feelings while pretending to have transcended them. However, as I progressed on my spiritual journey, I discovered a more mature path that involves accepting all aspects of myself, including what appear to be the dark and negative ones. I was wrong to assume that spiritual enlightenment could be attained while neglecting unresolved emotional issues or traumatic wounds. I learned that such issues and wounds hold crucial spiritual lessons that must be learned before reaching a profound awakening.

Many close friends and family members asked how I was doing during those darkest days. At first, I answered that I felt much better than expected. But that wasn't true. I was numb inside and lost for the first time in my life. This moment was becoming a real test of my spiritual practice.

So instead of pressuring myself to feel better, I decided to give myself permission to not be all right. I asked myself to embrace these difficult feelings and see this moment exactly as it was. I allowed myself to feel what was actually there, rather than trying to change it or running away from it.

When I made space for unprocessed emotions, I was soon able to notice the energy of rage in my body. It was like an intense fire, particularly around my chest and throat. I screamed in my room, and further expressed this rage through writing in a journal, therapeutic dancing, mountain climbing, and talking to trusted friends. After honoring my anger for a month or two, I allowed myself to feel deep grief and sorrow, to respect the part of me that felt like it had just died. I let all of the emotions that had been bottled up inside of me pour out in a torrent of tears. Eventually, after going through periods of rage, solitude, and tears, I found myself confronting the root of my emotions: fear.

In my journal, I asked my fear what I was afraid of. At first, it answered, "I am afraid of not being able to provide for those who have been dependent on me, like my aging parents, my godson, my assistants, my staff members, and their families." Then I asked again what I was really afraid of. After a moment of silence, I had a sudden flashback from my childhood while I was writing.

I was a little boy desperately looking for my mom in a big open market. I was overwhelmed with panic and scared to death. Several adults came up to me as I was in tears and asked, "Where is your mother? Did you lose her?" Then a strange old lady took my hand and told me that she would take me to my mom. I reluctantly went with her. When we arrived at her house, I saw only a scary man, not my mom. Sensing that something was terribly wrong, I escaped through an open door and ran back to the market as fast as I could. After frantically wandering through the market for a while, I finally saw my mom desperately looking for me.

At last, I understood why I had had the fear of abandonment all along. It originated from my suppressed trauma in early childhood. For a long time, I had been ignoring the frightened inner child who had been separated from a source of love, warmth, and security. The dark void I felt represented the scary world that little boy found himself in, without his mother. I could see why I had to go through my worst nightmare. It was all part of my journey to meet the little boy and to integrate the part that had been—up until that moment—too frightening to become conscious of. I took a deep breath and spoke to the little boy: "I see you now. I will always stay right here with you, and never ever abandon you. I accept you just as you are, and love you with my whole heart."

THINGS DON'T OFTEN HAPPEN IN our lives like we have hoped. When we encounter unfavorable outcomes, we often experience difficult emotions. If this is happening to you right now, no matter how overwhelming and terrifying it is, I want you to know that you can weather the storm. You are stronger than you feel right now and wiser than you believe.

Once the storm quiets down, and it will surely pass, don't feel the need to pick yourself up immediately and get right back to where you were before. Give yourself time to sit with your present feelings. Once you make time and space for your emotions, you will be able to process them easily and ask important questions such as "What am I feeling now?" "What are my emotions trying to tell me?" and "What did I learn from the experience?" When we pose these questions with curiosity, rather than with judgment, we will come to see deeper truths about ourselves.

This process will then help us to remain collected and respond wisely instead of reacting impulsively. We get to redefine who we truly are by the way we respond to a setback. Remember that the greatest stories are not the ones where everything goes smoothly, as expected; they are always the ones about overcoming hardship and bouncing back from failure.

We have not finished authoring the book of our lives yet. Let us write one of the most meaningful stories with no regret.

*

The greatest glory in living lies
not in never falling,
but in rising every time we fall.
—Nelson Mandela

*

Welcome your pain,
for it will make you see the truth.
Embrace your failure,
for it will serve as a catalyst for growth.
Love your inner chaos,
for it will lead to self-discovery.

*

Pain teaches life lessons,
pleasure doesn't.

*

I know you feel so alone and lost now.
But even in your darkest moments,
there is love to guide you through.
I will never give up on you.

*

Like the way the darkness brings out the stars,
you will be able to see who your true friends are
in the darkest moment of your life.

*

When you fall in a dark theater
give your eyes a moment to adjust before getting up.
Similarly, if life knocks you down,
take your time to process your emotions and wait for
a clear path forward to become visible.

*

We make peace with it
when we can understand it.

*

Processing emotions means making sense of one's feelings
by acknowledging their presence and understanding the cause.
As a result, one finds healthy ways to cope with them,
rather than being unconsciously controlled by them.

*

Don't be easily offended,
as what others say is often just a reflection of
their own feelings and limited experiences,
rather than an objective assessment of you.

*

When you judge another,
you do not define them.
You define yourself.
—Dr. Wayne W. Dyer

*

As you habitually talk about other people's problems,
you get stuck in that vibrational frequency,
attracting those problems to your own life.

*

Some may find your vulnerability brave,
while others may view it as overly emotional.
Some may think your assertiveness is charismatic,
while others may see it as selfish and overbearing.
Some may view your animated personality as interesting,
while others may find it annoying and disingenuous.
Keep in mind that trying to please everyone is pointless.

*

The only way to avoid criticism is
to do nothing, say nothing, and be nothing.
—Elbert Hubbard

*

Let it be okay to be disliked,
because no matter what you do,
there will always be someone who disapproves of you.
So instead of worrying about criticism and rejection,
make choices based on your values and needs
and always live your life authentically.

*

Don't seek validation from others.
Instead, take the journey of self-discovery
and let yourself be your own validator.
Reflect on your accomplishments and strengths,
appreciate your kindness and creativity, and
understand your true needs and values.
Develop a sense of self-worth that is
independent of other's opinions.

*

I like myself,
this soft, caring being inside,
ever attentive to the well-being of others,
wishing them to be loved and protected.

*

A sure-fire way to self-loathing:
pretending to be someone you aren't
in order to gain validation from others
while ignoring your own needs and wants.

*

If you have an anxious attachment style
and tend to put others' needs before your own,
for the sake of your well-being
don't just think about what you need,
but communicate your needs to others.

*

One doesn't become enlightened by
imagining figures of light,
but by making the darkness conscious.
—Carl Jung

*

The flaws that you see so frequently in others
are actually your inner conflicts and unwanted traits,
existing in the shadow of your unconsciousness.
Unless you bring them to light and accept them as part of you,
those annoying people won't disappear from your life.

*

Can you love me, the whole of me,
not just the part that makes you smile
but also the part that I am afraid to share?

*

If the ultimate goal of spiritual practice is
unconditional peace, then the path is not
that of self-improvement,
but of self-acceptance.

*

By accepting things as they are,
resistance subsides and peace emerges.
In that experience, there is no separate "I"
that stands apart and experiences peace.
"I" is never needed in peace.
"I" disappears in peace.

*

Still inside, still outside.
One undivided stillness
permeates the universe.

*

Enlightenment signifies
the deepest level of intimacy with the world,
where the individual no longer stands apart from it.

*

Since I've learned to be silent,
everything has come so much closer to me.
—Rainer Maria Rilke

# Why Are We Unhappy?

THE ANSWER IS RATHER SIMPLE. We are unhappy because we can't find peace with what is. We wish things to be different from what is happening at that moment. For instance, if we see something attractive or pleasant, our mind cannot remain calm. Rather, it is drawn toward the new object, wants to stay close to it and wishes to engage with it. If possible, we want to possess it completely and use it as we desire. The Buddha described this kind of mental pursuit as "grasping." When our mind is grasping at something, we feel unfulfilled until we have the object under our control. While sensing incompleteness, the mind is restless and dissatisfied.

Conversely, if we perceive something to be disagreeable or unpleasant, our mind wants to run away and avoid contact with it for as long as we can. If we must encounter it, we try to do so as briefly as possible. Unlike the grasping mind, the mind in this state is "resisting." The longer we resist, the more intolerable the situation becomes. We grow increasingly anxious and even angry since we can't walk away from it. Modern psychologists call this mental resistance "stress." When stressed, we are almost always resisting something—be it a person, object, or situation.

This is not to suggest that you should not resist things that make you miserable. Rather, I am simply pointing out the fact that it may not be the person, object, or situation in and of itself that is causing you to feel unhappy and stressed. If the unpleasant quality were intrinsic to the person, for instance, then that person would be deemed unpleasant by everyone, not just you personally. However, the degree to which someone is unpleasant varies widely among individuals; I might find him aggravating, while my friend thinks he is charming.

Then what is the true cause of our frequent unhappiness? The real culprit, in my opinion, is constant mental activity toward objects. As long as a mind swings back and forth—grasping for something you don't have and resisting something you already have—it will remain in a perpetual state of struggle and busyness. It will find a current situation subtly, or not so subtly, unsatisfying and problematic. Such a mind is often tensed, and lacking relaxed openness, acceptance, and self-awareness. If it doesn't turn inward and become aware of its habitual tendency to move away from a given situation, a mind will continue to jump from one object to the next—always blaming external things for its inner discomfort. Such a mind also demands that a person, object, or situation change to accommodate its preference since, according to this mind, the desired change is not just a better and sensible alternative but also the right course of action.

It is important to note here that I am not trying to condone people's bad behavior, as if we are to blame ourselves for feeling unhappy. My point is that the mind is an intermediary agent, interpreting how we feel about what is happening in the world around us. A raw experience is neither inherently good nor bad. It just is. Yet our minds are quick to judge and then interpret something as either pleasant or unpleasant. Not surprisingly, the same raw experience can be interpreted quite differently from person to person, as each individual has been uniquely conditioned depending upon their past experiences.

IF THIS IS INDEED THE CASE, what can we do to make our minds feel at peace and content, instead of ceaselessly grasping and resisting? Are there any practices with which we can better regulate our emotions and find equanimity and acceptance?

The most well-known practice for countering the mind's tendency to wander is gratitude. When we feel thankful, we usually don't think about what we don't have, or what we could have. This diminishes the mind's grasping tendency to want something else. At the same time, a grateful mind is open and receptive, so the resisting tendency of disliking what is here is also diminished. As we become glad about what has happened in the past and grateful for what we already have right now, our mind becomes calm and peaceful, unlike a resisting mind that is often full of critical thoughts, complaints, or arguments. When our heart is filled with thankfulness, there is little to no room for such negative thoughts.

When we practice gratitude, we can acknowledge not only what we are fortunate enough to have, including health, a job, a home, clothes, nice weather, and so on, but also what others have provided for us to maintain our good lives. For instance, we can be grateful for a parent's continuous support, a friend's wicked humor, or a partner's warm hug. We can also say "thank you" to ourselves for not giving up in the face of multiple rejections, for picking ourselves up after heartbreak. The more we practice gratitude, the more we will come to appreciate and be thankful for the things we have.

To practice gratitude, look for three to five things a day to be thankful for and send a text message to yourself or a "gratitude buddy," someone willing to exchange grateful experiences. Another idea is to pick up a beautiful pebble and place it somewhere visible in your home. Every time you pass and look at the pebble, search your mind for one thing to be grateful for at that moment. You could also take a photo every time you feel thankful, and share it with friends and family. Or you could make a habit out of saying a heartfelt "thank you" quietly or out loud to those who assist you at a restaurant, supermarket, coffee shop, or gas station, or on a bus or train.

Another way to counteract the mind's restless tendency is to wholeheartedly welcome unhappy experiences. Since our emotional well-being is primarily determined not so much by the present situation but rather our response to it, we can reduce our suffering by intentionally switching from the impulse to resist to a welcoming attitude. Rather than thinking that those uncomfortable situations shouldn't be here, as if they were anomalies, we should include them as a part of our everyday default settings. Instead of praying that difficult situations never arise, we should not only expect to experience them but also welcome them. That way, when they occur, we won't feel surprised or even upset because we know that they are and always will be part and parcel of our lives.

As for actual practices, while brushing your teeth or washing your face in the morning, spend one minute telling your mind a few times, "Bring on discomfort! I will accept you gladly." Having primed your mind to anticipate an uncomfortable situation early on, and having made your intention to accept it clear, you will be ready when you actually run into it. Of course, if the situation is life-threateningly uncomfortable, remove yourself from it as swiftly as possible. But if the situation is not life-threatening, just unavoidable, you can become mindful of your inclination to resist it and adopt a welcoming attitude by repeating this affirmation, "Bring on discomfort! I will accept you gladly." Then, when that uncomfortable situation arises, count backward—"three, two, one"—and march right into it without any hesitation.

We can also have a more accepting relationship with unhappiness by reminding ourselves that the universe wants us to grow from the pain of unhappy experiences. When every situation is agreeable and pleasant, we have no reason to grow into a more mature version of ourselves. Only when we move out of our comfort zone and find ourselves in the space of unfamiliarity and discomfort do we begin to learn and expand intellectually, emotionally, and spiritually. According to the thirteenth-century Persian poet Rumi, "The wound is the place where the light enters you." Instead of turning away from our wounds, we should examine them closely and discover the hidden light of gratitude, acceptance, and wisdom.

*

We human beings have two sides.
Our "human" side is bustling with the commotion of life,
emotions fluctuating and thoughts a jumbled mess.
Our "being" side is a serene presence, untethered by time,
watching the mind and the world unfold with stillness.
The mystery is that these two are one and the same.

*

What if the path to happiness is not
bringing order to the mess of our lives,
but instead relaxing amid the mess
and rejoicing in its aliveness and beauty?

*

Happiness is not a state to arrive at,
but a manner of traveling.*
—Margaret Lee Runbeck

*

No matter how good your environment,
if you are always longing for something else,
you will never be happy.
This is because happiness arises
when our minds stop being restless
and begin to accept and appreciate what is.

*

According to a Korean Buddhist adage,
we are advised to:
"Neither hinder those who seek to come,
nor grasp those who wish to leave."
By embracing an attitude of acceptance,
we can avoid needless heartaches and wasted efforts,
and instead, find peace in the natural flow of life.

*

When you are struggling, notice that
it is not the situation itself
but your psychological resistance to it
that causes your pain.
You can ease this resistance
by imagining that the given situation
was actually your choice.
Believe that it was part of
your soul's plan for growth.
And then observe what happens.

*

When people accept themselves just as they are,
they are more likely to change for the better.
Until then, they remain defensive, resist feedback,
and rationalize why they cannot change.

*

God, grant me the serenity
to accept the things I cannot change,
the courage to change the things I can,
and the wisdom to know the difference.
—Reinhold Niebuhr

*

Acceptance doesn't mean excusing bad behavior
or making what happened to you okay. Instead,
it means letting go of your wish to change the past, and
inviting peace to your heart so that you can focus on
what truly matters to you in the present moment.

*

To let go does not mean to get rid of.
To let go means to let be.
When we let be with compassion,
things come and go on their own.
—Jack Kornfield

*

As long as I am chasing something,
I remain unfulfilled and bound.
There is no contentment, freedom, or peace.

*

Wise individuals cultivate contentment with what they have,
making them not easily swayed by temptation or pressure,
enabling them to pursue only what they truly desire.

*

The more confident I am,
the more magnetic I become.
The less attached I am,
the less control others have over me.

*

At your school reunion, you encounter
someone you were once infatuated with,
only to find them to be just an average person.
You wonder why you were so captivated by them,
and how you saw them as being so exceptional.
Then you realize that it wasn't their inherent qualities
but rather your intense attachment and obsessive thinking
that made them appear unique and different.

*

Remember the most difficult time of your life,
marked by loss, illness, heartbreak, or uncertainty.
Didn't you just wish for it to end soon?
Now take a moment to appreciate
how far you have come and
feel grateful for this peaceful time.

*

Before giving you fresh attire,
the universe will first empty out your wardrobe.
If you have experienced great difficulties,
see what happens in the next phase of your life.

*

Out of suffering have emerged
the strongest souls;
the most massive characters are
seared with scars.
—Edwin Hubbell Chapin

*

There comes a time in our lives
when we realize that everything we have
can be taken away in the blink of an eye.
Let us stay thankful and
never take anything for granted.

*

Take note of all the blessings you have received.
Jot them down and, as you reflect, bask in
feelings of abundance, gratitude, and security.
Let these wonderful feelings permeate every cell
of your being and stay with you throughout the day.

*

I am grateful for the nice sunny weather today.
I am grateful that I am in relatively good health.
I am grateful that I have loving family and friends.
I am grateful that I can relish this warm cup of coffee.

*

Gratitude can transform
common days into thanksgivings,
turn routine jobs into joy, and
change ordinary opportunities into blessings.*
—William Arthur Ward

*

Just as we take a daily vitamin supplement,
let's take the potent "gratitude pill" by counting
our blessings every morning. It will shield us from
negative emotions, boost our physical health,
enhance our relationships, and uplift our spirits.

*

While renovating a physical space takes time,
changing the ambience of our mind can be done
instantly by shifting to positive thoughts.
By intentionally having desirable thoughts
and dwelling on the good feelings they evoke,
we create a mental environment we want to inhabit.

*

If you want to hear easy-listening music,
just tune your radio to the right frequency.
If you want to live a prosperous life,
adjust your mindset to focus on gratitude and giving.
This will attract more blessings to come your way,
much like easy-listening music continues to
play on the same radio frequency.

*

Pray not from a place of scarcity
but from a mindset of abundance and gratitude,
as the universe is more likely to respond to
what you are, not what you want.

*

You will be surprised by how many things
you can receive by simply asking nicely, including
those you may have thought were out of reach.
You just have to be willing to ask for them.

*

Don't force people to achieve your goals,
as the best results always come
when they occur naturally
with a sense of ease and flow.

*

The great mystery is that your desires are
partially realized in the moment you think of them.
Therefore, act as if you have already achieved them.
This way, you attract them instead of chasing after them.
This is a shortcut to fulfilling your desires.

*

According to Buddhist teachings,
psychology is equivalent to cosmology.
If your mind is filled with loving-kindness,
you experience heaven.
If it is overflowing with hatred and anger,
you experience hell.
Both heaven and hell are created by
and experienced with your mind,
making them inseparable.

# How Do You Feel About the Universe?

Do you feel that the universe is abundant and benevolent or scarce and uncaring? I'm not talking about how you think about the universe in a scientific sense, but rather, how you feel about it in your gut. Do you feel that the universe has been looking after you, always providing you with a new friend, love, job, money, or house when you honestly ask for it? Or do you feel that the universe is a meaningless dead space where all living beings must compete for limited resources and fend for themselves to survive? Can you completely trust the universe to guide you in the right direction and deliver what you need? Or do you feel that life is a zero-sum game where someone's success is unfortunately your loss, and there is no such thing as a benevolent force or higher power beyond this world?

Don't feel perplexed if you are not sure how you truly feel about the universe. It is quite possible for your mind to like the idea that it is abundant and benevolent while your gut is feeling quite the opposite way. Whatever feeling you have about the universe is important because it will determine not only your general outlook on life and human relationships but also how easily you will be able to navigate a difficult time.

As you might have guessed, the formation of this feeling has a lot to do with how we were raised as children, and how people in general were treated in our community. If our needs were met most of the time and we were treated kindly, we are more likely to feel that we can trust the universe. In contrast, if we were treated badly, we find ourselves having a hard time developing that trust. Interestingly, this feeling is often hereditary, passing from one generation to the next on a subconscious level. When I first examined my own case, I was surprised to find out how much I had internalized my own father's feeling without fully realizing it.

My father has been incredibly caring and supportive throughout my life. When he was young, he made a conscious decision not to be like my grandfather. My grandfather was popular and well-regarded in the wider community, but an unreliable breadwinner and irresponsible caretaker at home. He showed little attention or love to any of his six children except for his eldest son, my father's older brother.

To make matters worse, my father was born right before the Korean War, when most Korean families lacked enough food, not to mention other necessities. My father told me that if he wanted to eat another potato after his first one, he had to eat faster than all his siblings. He spent many lunch breaks just drinking water to fill up his empty stomach as my grandmother couldn't afford to pack lunches for all her children. Life was tough for him as he didn't receive enough care and support—be it in terms of food, shoes, education, or attention from his parents.

Consequently, for my father, the universe was a place of scarcity. He felt that unless he struggled to get what he needed, no one would come and give it to him. This feeling led him to become a diligent and responsible man who provided for his wife and two sons. On the other hand, he didn't fully trust people outside his immediate family and wasn't particularly kind to them either. This bothered me a lot, particularly during my adolescent years. My father was very warm at home but often cold and uncaring to others outside the family.

When I was ordained in my midtwenties, I formed a special relationship with another important father figure in my life: my monastic teacher. In the Buddhist monastic community, this relationship is very much like the one between a father and a son. He was the one who sponsored my ordination and trained me to be a monk. When he passes, I will be the one who organizes his funeral and takes care of his ashes.

Interestingly, my teacher's view of the universe is quite the opposite of my father's. He has an unshakable trust in the universe or, in his world view, the Buddha. It has been his experience that, although it may take some time, he always receives what he needs after praying—be that donations, volunteers, professional help for the temple's various needs, or even good weather for the Buddha's birthday celebrations. He has a very relaxed and accepting attitude toward life.

He also believes that there are more than enough "pies" to go around for everyone. Because of this belief, he is naturally very generous as he frequently gives away whatever he owns to whoever asks for it. Nine times out of ten, he picks up the check before anyone else—even when dining with wealthy people. He often splits the personal donations he sometimes receives with other monks and nuns. I am blessed to have a teacher like him and admire his generous heart and deep faith in the Buddha. Among many things, he has shown me what my father couldn't: how to trust the universe and live life accordingly.

When I first read the Bible in my teens, there was one passage that stood out: Jesus taught his disciples in Matthew 6:25 not to worry about whether they had enough food or clothes, as God would surely provide them with whatever they needed. Given that wild birds find enough food without having to store it away, and fields of grass are clothed with splendid flowers without any labor, he said, why do you worry that you won't be provided for? Reflecting on these verses now, I think Jesus was essentially asking his followers to change their view of the universe from one of scarcity and indifference to one of abundance and benevolence through cultivating faith.

For many people, including myself, it can be quite daunting to make a leap of faith completely. It is often because a feeling of distrust has been planted deeply in our guts since childhood, originating from our parents and grandparents. Even if we wholeheartedly agree that the universe is a place of abundance and benevolence, we might still need time to fully assimilate this idea and live our lives accordingly. As I count my blessings each day, and see many great examples shown by my teacher and others, I feel increasingly comfortable about letting go of my control and inviting grace into my life. As I find more instances of grace, I become more relaxed and appreciative, discovering even more wonderful gifts this universe has sent my way.

When we go through a difficult period in our lives, allowing our heart to trust the universe can be enormously helpful. Even if we don't get the job this time, or are rejected by a romantic interest, we have faith that the universe will guide us to the right one soon. We can congratulate other people's success because we know that we will have other opportunities to create our own version of success as well. We can choose to forgive those who have wronged us and move on because, once we do that, the universe will open a new chapter of our lives for us. Even if a family member or close friend passes away, we can trust that they aren't alone and will be received by the universe with kindness and compassion.

Ultimately, this is a choice we need to make. We can decide what kind of universe we would like to live in. Buddhism teaches that each individual experiences an entirely different kind of universe based on that person's state of mind. As we engage in more benevolent thoughts and acts, we will naturally experience a more benevolent universe. Of course, the opposite is also true. Given that we have this power to create our own universe, as opposed to believing that we are just the product of our circumstances, how will you choose to feel about the universe and work with your power?

Chapter 2

# When Your Heart Is Aching

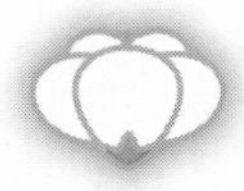

# Please Reject Me Gently!

I CAN SEE WHY PEOPLE say a job interview is like a first date. Here I was, nervously waiting to have my first coffee "date" with the department head of the college where I had been shortlisted for a tenure-track assistant professor position. For the next three days of my campus interview, I was scheduled not only to give a public lecture of my research but also to go out with potential future colleagues for meals or afternoon-coffee "dates." I was to establish rapport quickly with them and create a positive impression while assessing what it would be like to work together in the same department.

When I finally sat down with my first "date" in the campus cafe, I found her to be cordial and kind. Sitting there with a warm cup of chai latte in my hands, I relaxed and answered her casual-sounding yet important questions. She asked where I had studied before, how I had become interested in my research topic, and what my future plan was at that time. I then inquired what made the college unique and what her recent academic interests were. It became obvious that she wanted me to have a favorable impression of the college just as much as I wished her to choose me over the other two finalists.

After spending three days on the campus as a potential colleague, I started to bond with some of the faculty members and became truly excited about the prospect of teaching there. I even investigated a few potential apartments in the college town and began to imagine what my daily routine would be like as an assistant professor. Like a teenager who had just returned home from his first date, I couldn't stop thinking about my experiences there and felt as if I was about to fall in love with that place. Like any good date would do, I promptly sent a thank-you message after arriving at my home city and patiently waited for a call.

About four weeks later, I finally received the message that I had been waiting for. It was not a phone call, but a short email instead. The department head shared how much she had enjoyed my visit to the campus and was impressed by my work. However, the search committee had unfortunately decided to select another candidate because that person was a better "fit" for the college's needs. She wished me luck with my job search. The tone of her email—unlike the time of our first meeting—felt devoid of warmth and seemed formulaic, as if the same email had been sent to the other candidate that they didn't select too.

I was devastated. It felt as though someone had thrown a bucket of ice-cold water over my head. It turned out that my burgeoning love was only the unrequited kind. I could hear my critical inner voice belittling my intellect, appearance, and English accent while doubting my future as a college professor. I began reviewing my visit, wondering what I had done wrong. There were a lot of thoughts of regret, starting with "I should've" and "I could've." Even though everyone told me not to, I took the rejection personally. I couldn't help but think that they had chosen someone else because I wasn't good enough.

As I continued with my job search, however, I noticed something quite unexpected. Job interviews were like any other skill in life: the more I practiced, the better I got. By the time I was on my third on-campus interview, I was noticeably less nervous and more confident and personable in my interactions with the people I met. I already knew how to answer most of the typical questions posed by the committee. I understood more clearly their needs and could talk extensively about how I could satisfy them. One place was looking for a candidate well-trained in postmodern cultural theories, while another place wanted a medieval historian capable of teaching both Buddhism and medieval East Asian history. Each college was looking for a uniquely shaped piece that would fit neatly into their existing mold.

Then the reason I shouldn't take the rejection too personally dawned on me: the decision to choose one candidate over another had less to do with a candidate's qualifications and more to do with the varying desires of the committee, who had specific biases, preferences, and unique histories.

Going forward, I also didn't make the same mistake of falling in love too quickly. Rather than daydreaming about my future in any place, I brought my attention to the present moment and focused on what I needed to do *now*. Whenever I met an interviewer for coffee or a meal, I remained friendly, sincere, and collected. After much trial and error, I eventually had the phone call I was waiting for and received a job offer from a respected liberal arts college.

WHETHER WE'RE TURNED DOWN BY a romantic interest, blocked by a friend on social media or didn't get the promotion we've been aiming for, rejection always hurts. It lowers our self-esteem and awakens the critical inner voice. We can easily become angry, sad, and insecure while ruminating on our shortcomings. If you are struggling with emotional pain after rejection, my heart goes out to you as I've had to deal with it many times in my life. In this moment of difficulty, I would like to offer you the following advice.

First, there is no need to take rejection personally. Each person has unique tastes and preferences shaped by their own history. Those things were already formed long before meeting you. Therefore, if people reject you, it has much to do with their experiences and individual tastes. In addition, people subconsciously prefer what they are familiar with. Even if you are objectively the best candidate as a lover, friend, or employee, you won't be liked if you appear unfamiliar. This, however, doesn't diminish your value and self-worth. You are still talented, kind, and likable. All your good qualities are still there. It simply means that you and the person who rejected you are not the right match for each other.

Second, ask yourself whether you haven't rejected some people in your own life. Haven't you declined an offer to go out on a date with someone? Haven't you broken someone's heart? Haven't you blocked certain people on social media? It is ridiculous to expect that everyone you like will always like you back. It is simply impossible. What is equally absurd is arriving at the other extreme assumption: that just because some people have rejected me, I must be unlikable and will never be able to find true love, friendship, or my dream job. This, of course, is nonsense. If you are patient and willing to continue with your effort despite some setbacks, you will eventually find what you are looking for.

Third, rejection can be a distressing experience that can leave us feeling unwanted and undervalued. When we experience rejection, it is important to surround ourselves with people who appreciate and love us. Sharing our difficult experiences with trusted friends and family can help us to alleviate the intensity of our negative emotions and feel validated. There is a saying in Korean that "Joy shared doubles the joy while sorrow shared halves the sorrow," which highlights the importance of talking about our experiences. Therefore, it is better to reach out and talk to others instead of trying to cope with emotional pain alone.

My last advice is to take time to reflect on your experiences and continue to move forward. When you encounter rejection, allow yourself to process your emotions and regain your composure. Then, take a moment to think about what you can learn from the experience, as there is no better teacher than real-life situations. Internalize the lessons you learn and apply them to your next opportunity. Remember that finding the right path may require many attempts. It may take much trial and error. But if you regard rejection as an opportunity to grow, you will eventually find the path that works for you and arrive at a destination you will be content with. I am rooting for you!

*

Don't be discouraged by rejection:
an even better path may lie ahead.
What may seem like a setback often
turns out to be a blessing in disguise.

*

If you could go back ten years and
offer one piece of advice to your younger self,
it would probably be something like:
"Don't worry, it will all work out."
Now listen to the same advice from your future self:
"Trust me, no need to worry. It did all work out."

*

They rejected only your application.
They didn't reject you as a person.
They made that decision because it wasn't
suitable for their unique circumstances;
it wasn't a reflection of you.

*

People choose what is familiar,
even if it will only perpetuate pain,
because that is the only devil they know.

*

If your idea is rejected,
take the initiative and start small,
doing it your own way.
Although your start may be slow,
as you gain experience and skills
no one will be able to discredit you,
and your success will be enduring.

*

I know it hurts to be treated like that.
Your future self can make them regret
not showing you more kindness and respect
when they had the opportunity.

*

It is said that those who are patient
will be blessed in the end.
When something is testing your patience,
take a deep breath and think:
"Ah, this has happened so that I might be blessed!"

*

Wonderful things in life take time,
like artisan cheese, flavorful red wine, delicious kimchi,
thriving coral reefs, bountiful vegetable gardens, lush flower fields,
deep trust, strong relationships, financial security, and
a fulfilling career.

*

When evaluating someone's achievements,
we tend to focus on their personal accomplishments.
However, it is just as crucial to consider
the positive impact they have had on others,
such as helping others to achieve their own dreams.

*

Happiness
is seeing someone that I have helped
become successful and happy.

*

One thing that you must avoid
if you want to achieve great success:
following others blindly without developing
your own style and approach.
One thing that you must avoid
when you have already succeeded:
arrogance.

*

He who is overconfident in his abilities
believes that he can do things even better than the experts.
In extreme cases, he even tries to teach the experts.
This is a grave mistake, and a foolish thing to do.

*

Those who proudly claim to have the best and the finest in the world
may not yet have had the opportunity to explore
the richness of other cultures, perspectives, and life experiences.
If they did, they would have said that what they have
may not be the global best, but it is their personal best.

*

If your date says they don't want a relationship,
believe them and move on. Don't try to convince
them otherwise by showing how great you are.
Save that for someone who wants a relationship.

*

If the person you have been dating is ghosting you,
send a light-hearted message directly addressing the situation.
Try saying, "Have I been ghosted, Casper?" and see what happens.

*

Avoid ghosting and be honest in your communication.
If it is not working, send a clear and simple message like,
"Thank you for your time, but I don't think
we are a match unfortunately. Wishing you all the best!"
This saves time, energy, and prevents unnecessary heartache.

*

Beware of a bitter or blaming tone
when discussing past relationships,
as it can predict future behavior.

*

If you can't make it at the suggested time,
don't just decline.
Offer an alternative time that works for you,
unless ending the relationship is your intention.

✳

If you feel like you are on the verge of a mental breakdown
due to constant belittlement and harassment from someone,
then keep in mind this truth:
there is something wrong with that person, not you.
People who like themselves do not mistreat others like that.
Regardless of what the person says, do not take it personally.

✳

We cannot be responsible for other people's unhappiness,
especially when we have not caused it.
Maintain a respectful attitude toward others
while setting clear boundaries.
If you are increasingly unhappy as you try to help someone,
your initial good intentions may transform into resentment.

*

The higher a person's self-esteem,
the more they respect others, and the kinder they are to people.
Those who look down on others and treat them as unimportant
either never experienced being respected while growing up
or feel that they themselves are unimportant now.

*

In life, we sometimes find ourselves in a situation
where there is nothing much we can do for our loved one in pain.
At times like this, try to maintain a tranquil outlook
instead of losing your mind in sadness and despair.
Your calm gaze will be a source of great strength to that person.

*

When we take care of aging parents, we need to remember
that all of us made unreasonable demands and asked
the same questions over and over when we were children.
Our parents, too, surely wanted to live their own lives,
but they sacrificed their time for us.
They already did it for us; what are we doing for them now?

*

It is not that we don't understand the truth of impermanence.
It's just that we sometimes forget this while vaguely thinking that
our loved ones will somehow remain with us always.
But when we lose them, it surprises us and breaks our hearts.

*

When we experience the loss of someone important,
we can blame the world and close the door of our heart
in order to protect ourselves from pain. Alternatively,
we can also honor the loss with an open heart and love
and connect with those who share our grief and loneliness.

*

When parents pass away, and
their wealth is divided among children,
if you are not careful, you can cause
a lot of hurt and misunderstanding.
What would your deceased parents say if they found out that
their children had stopped talking to one another
because of the inheritance?
May you have the wisdom to know how to curb your greed and
live the rest of your life not estranged but on good terms
with your siblings.

*

No matter how much wealth there might be,
if you argue over it, it will seem small.
On the other hand, if you care for one another,
even a single piece of bread divided will leave leftovers.

*

There is a Buddhist saying that "love has no enemy."
If you would like to protect yourself in this scary world,
have a heart of love that does not hate others.
It is difficult to harm someone who truly loves you.

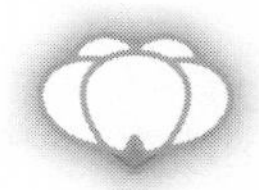

# Spring Days Are Gone

In the late 90s, I got on a train to Princeton University for the first time in my life. I could feel the excitement of the upcoming spring in the crisp March breeze. I was heading there to visit the campus after having been accepted on to the doctoral program. My heart was brimming with anticipation and nervousness about the people I was about to meet.

As the train arrived at Princeton Station, I stepped down on to the platform and looked for Jason, a graduate student from the same department, who had agreed to meet me there. Jason spotted me immediately and walked over. He was about my height and age and had a kind appearance. I soon felt comfortable with him, as though I had known him for a long time. He had studied in Japan for many years and understood Asian culture well. For the three days and two nights of my visit, I imposed on Jason and stayed in his dorm room. We talked quite a bit about the doctoral program and the living situation in

Princeton. Thanks to his detailed answers and the wonderful professors I met, I didn't take up the offers of the other universities and decided to attend Princeton.

Before I began my doctoral program, Jason told me that he would not be staying in the dormitories the following semester. He planned to move to a two-bedroom graduate apartment and asked me if I wanted to share the place with him. At the thought of being able to start a new life not on my own but with a friend like Jason, I gladly agreed. We moved into the new apartment a few weeks before the semester was to begin. We bought desks, bookshelves, and the kitchen utensils that we would be sharing. We often made dinners together, went to weekend concerts, and even occasionally attended Dharma talks at my teacher's temple near New York. Although it had only been a few weeks, we became close friends, which made me very happy.

Once the semester started, though, we were both busy with our own classes. I had to continue my study of Chinese and Japanese, in addition to my major coursework, and Jason began to study the Korean he had been wanting to learn. So it was only natural that I frequently asked Jason about Japan, while he did the same with me regarding Korea. As time went on, though, I realized that we thought quite differently on certain subjects. For example, when we discussed politics, we had different views about world leaders and their policies. He would sometimes take the side of a leader or a policy I didn't agree with, and vice versa. We would passionately discuss the topic late into the night, and surprisingly, we sometimes ended up with hurt feelings over seemingly trivial matters.

In situations like this, if people spend a few days away from each other and give each other some psychological space, they often come to realize that the thing they disagreed on is not such a big deal after all, and things return to normal. But since it was just Jason and me in that small apartment, it was difficult to give each other that space. To make matters worse, we often shared our ride to the campus, so the awkwardness between us would last for quite some time.

Other disagreements with Jason arose from things that I couldn't have imagined. At the time, whenever I cooked rice, I would make enough so that Jason could have some as well, using the keep-warm function on my electric rice cooker. I usually made two or three days' worth of rice at one time, but for some reason, Jason would not touch day-old rice. When I asked him why, he told me that he didn't like old rice, no matter how warm it was kept. Before I knew it, we were in a somewhat absurd situation of both owning individual rice cookers in our tiny kitchen and cooking rice separately. In the end, though we lived in the same apartment, it became rarer and rarer for us to sit down together for a meal and talk.

The autumn semester ended, and at the beginning of the spring semester the following year, Jason and I raised our voices at each other. Jason had bought a new camera, and I had mistaken the instruction manual for rubbish and thrown it out. In general, I preferred to live minimally and thus liked to throw things away, while Jason was inclined to keep mementos and preserve important documents and books. I apologized to him for my carelessness, but a period of silence and quiet tension lingered between us for some time after that. When we eventually resumed talking, it was only after things had become too awkward between us to bear.

Anyone who has ever experienced living with a roommate will know that the relationship can go awry over the tiniest of things. What may not have been a big deal when you were just friends can quickly become a source of tension and resentment when sharing living space. For example, you might have different ways of doing the dishes or cleaning the bathroom, or you might have different tastes in the music or the television shows you like to watch. Other factors such as different bedtimes, snoring during sleep, or frequent visits from friends can also potentially lead to problems. It is hard to predict where conflicts may arise, even if the person is your best friend or romantic partner. If you live with someone you don't know at all, it is easier to maintain the level of courtesy and indifference needed not to intrude on each other's lives. However, this is not possible for people who already know each other well.

Jiddu Krishnamurti, a great Indian spiritual teacher of the twentieth century, once said that we only come to know who we are through the mirror of relationships. That is, only when we observe how our mind responds in relationships do we discover our tendencies, pretensions, fears, desires, and vulnerabilities. Osho Rajneesh, another Indian teacher, said that to achieve maturity we do not need to make our hearts as hard as rocks and feel no pain. But rather the opposite is true: we should have the courage to face our own pain and the pains of others. By sensitizing ourselves to the realities of suffering and accepting it, we deepen our understanding of it and allow our mind to mature.

My relationship with Jason served as a mirror, reflecting back to me aspects of myself that I had previously been blind to. It was humbling to see my own selfish, ungenerous, and petty tendencies, which had gone unnoticed before. At the same time, I was deeply saddened and sorry for the way our friendship was unfolding. I spent those spring days of my midtwenties undergoing this process of self-reflection, during which I experienced a lot of heartache, sorrow, and regret.

IF YOU ARE MOVING IN with someone for the first time, whether as a roommate or a romantic partner, there are a few things I learned to avoid future conflicts.

First, give each other plenty of space. Although you may have enjoyed each other's company a lot before moving in, it is important to remember that you don't need to do everything together. Talk about what activities you want to do together and when you would like to be on your own. By giving each other space, you can pursue your individual interests without sacrificing your needs for the other person. When you spend too much time together without personal space, it can lead to feelings of suffocation and resentment, which can cause a lot of tension. By having some time to recharge and regroup, you can maintain a healthy balance, leading to a happier relationship.

Second, openly communicate about each other's expectations, particularly when it comes to living arrangements and finances. For example, who will take out the trash, or how thoroughly should the bathroom be cleaned? Will you do the laundry together or separately? Will you split the monthly rent and bills equally, or proportionally to each person's income or usage? Will you have a joint household expense account for food, or shop and pay separately? Is it ok to eat a yogurt or protein bar that is not yours and replace it later? Discussing these topics shortly after moving in can prevent frustration and resentment later.

Third, living with someone else means you may need to adjust your daily routine to live harmoniously. For example, if your roommate or partner likes to wake up early and you prefer to sleep in, you may need to compromise on when to turn off the lights at night or turn down the TV volume. You may have different dietary preferences, such as being lactose intolerant or vegetarian while the other person eats everything. In these situations, compromising and finding a way to cook that satisfies both parties is important.

Last, learn to raise an issue respectfully if your roommate

or partner upsets you. Everyone has their unique quirks, idiosyncratic habits, and pet peeves. Rather than bottling it up inside every time the other person does something that bothers you, communicate kindly and respectfully. It is highly likely that your roommate or partner does it unknowingly and unintentionally. By approaching these challenges with patience, empathy, and respect, you can create a harmonious living environment and build a stronger relationship.

*

Self-awareness is possible
through the mirror of relationships.
If you closely observe how your mind reacts
as you meet and converse with others,
you will come to understand who you are.

*

Spending time with good friends is very special
because, unlike other meetings in our lives,
this has no other purpose or hidden agenda.
Enjoying each other's company is the purpose.

*

A truly happy moment in this world:
when you meet a close friend after a long time apart
and spend the night catching up with each other.

*

Make it one of your life goals to make ten close friends.
Having close friends can have more of a lasting influence
on health and happiness than having success or accolades.
Just as we need nature as a place of refuge beyond our home,
so are friends essential to our lives in addition to our family.

*

If families are sent from heaven,
then friends are the family you choose.
—Jess C. Scott

*

The young ladies at the next table were all so happy
for their friend, saying "Wonderful!" over and over again
when she told them she had finally found a job.
I, even as a total stranger, became happy for her too.

*

A good friend is a magician—
the one who can easily double my happiness.

*

They say that the chance of laughter is thirty times higher
when you are with friends than when you are alone.
We laugh only fifteen percent of the time
because of something that was truly funny,
while the rest of the time we laugh
because those around us are laughing.
Laughter is the glue that holds relationships together.

*

Social gatherings can be divided into two types:
ones where the conversation is mostly about those who aren't there,
and those where people openly share their own experiences.
I find the latter type to be much more enjoyable.

*

Thank you for still being my friend
even after knowing my flaws and problems.
I am fortunate to have you in my life.

*

The moment you find fault with someone,
the similar flaw that has been dormant inside of you
wakes and starts to grow in you.
Don't water the seeds of your negativity.

*

If you think about it, we feel that other people are stubborn
probably because we, too, have that same stubbornness.
If we are not stubborn, we would simply see others as
people with conviction and drive.

*

One of the easiest things in the world to do
is to talk about the mistakes of others.
One of the hardest things in the world to do
is to look deeply into our own mistakes.

*

When you meet a new friend,
rather than trying to appear perfect or funny,
be courageous and show your genuine self.
They will feel that much closer to you.

*

In the process of getting close to people,
you are bound to have some disagreement with them.
Rather than running away at the first sign of conflict,
talk about the disagreement and try to reconcile the differences.
If you do, your relationship will take deeper roots.

*

When you first meet someone you like,
it is common to form an idealized
image of them based on your own desires.
However, as you get to know them better,
you may realize that they are not what you expected.
It is important to remember that this entire experience
took place within your own mind. They never
asked for you to have a positive view of them,
nor did they intend to let you down.

*

We often confuse "He is like that"
with "I wish he were like that."
In doing so, we mistakenly create
our own expectations and eventually
end up disappointed.

✳

Even if you have argued with someone,
once a certain period of time has passed and you have calmed down,
approach that person first and try to talk to them.
"How have you been? I regret the harsh things I said to you."
The mature person knows when to apologize and seeks to reconcile.

✳

If you confide in a friend about your struggles
and then later regret it,
even promising yourself never to do it again,
it is probably because you experienced judgment
rather than acceptance from your friend.
The issue lies in your friend's lack of empathy, not in you.
You showed courage by opening up and being vulnerable.

*

If you attempt to show understanding for your friend's struggles
by sharing your own comparable experience,
emphasizing how much tougher you had it,
that offers no solace.
What your friend needs now
is someone who asks about their feelings and listens attentively,
not someone who robs them of the opportunity to talk.

*

It doesn't help much to tell a struggling friend,
"Shake it off and move on!"
They, too, want to shake it off,
but they can't—that's why they are struggling.
Instead, tell them: "I can't imagine
what you just went through. I am here for you."

*

When circumstances require you to be around
those who make you feel uncomfortable,
use the experience as a learning opportunity.
Remind yourself to not exhibit similar behavior.
Also reflect on why you feel uneasy around them.
Is it because they trigger a past memory or wound?
Is it because they mirrored the repressed part in your shadow?
By understanding the source of your discomfort,
you can work on healing and growing as a person.

*

If you put a fancy flower like a rose in your living room,
it tends to wither away within several days. In contrast,
wildflowers with simple beauty often last much longer.
Our connection with someone who has splendid talent and looks
may seem very nice at first, but often doesn't last long.
On the other hand, building a relationship with someone
who lives modestly and reliably can lead to a long-lasting bond.

*

I think we change the course of our lives
far more from chance meetings with people
than from reading books or studying in school.
If you want to change your life, meet new people.

*

When I meet a good friend,
his positive reaction to me
makes me like myself more.

*

Some people go to priests;
others to poetry;
I to my friends.
—Virginia Woolf

# My Jealousy, My Suffering

When I was young, every time I returned from visiting my eldest uncle, I felt down for an extended period. This was due to the stark contrast between his luxurious apartment, with five bedrooms and two bathrooms, located in an affluent neighborhood with the best schools in Seoul, and my own family's rented shabby studio apartment. His place seemed like a completely foreign world to me, with its own distinct atmosphere and culture.

The smell was the first thing I noticed. When I opened the door to his apartment and stepped inside, I was greeted by a mysterious and warm fragrance, unlike that in my home. Immediately inside the door, the space next to the shoe cupboard was filled with all the things I had always wanted to play with—a basketball, a volleyball, a bicycle—and in the living room were a large, comfortable sofa and paintings by famous artists hanging on the walls. What I envied most was the room with the piano, something I wanted to learn so badly but had not been able to because we didn't have the money for lessons. The sight of my father's older brother and his family residing in such a gorgeous and spacious home felt like an elusive dream to me.

Living with my uncle were my two cousins, but—perhaps because they had spent some years living abroad—it felt as if a great river flowed between us. The two cousins simply stood on the opposite bank, making no effort to extend their hands and invite my younger brother and me to join them. So even when we visited my uncle, I only ever played with my own brother. You may wonder why I couldn't approach my cousins with warmth, but it was difficult for someone with little to extend a hand to someone with so much. I was also young, and it was my uncle's house, not my own, so I just hovered on the outskirts and went home feeling an inexplicable sense of sadness and loss.

Now that I am an adult, I am free of my complex about living with so little and can talk more easily about this. But in my youth, my uncle's magnificent home had a profound effect on me, evoking a sense of insignificance that was overwhelming and difficult to overcome, leading to a lingering resentment toward my parents for quite some time. Even though I was a very good student, my marks would always fall short of those of my older cousin, who was first in his entire grade. As I continued to experience these moments of wounded pride, I developed a deep sense of inferiority. No matter how hard I fought on my own in my inadequate home environment, it felt as if I would never be able to conquer the mountain that was my cousins.

Everyone must have at least one or two scenes from their

childhood that they can still see vividly when they close their eyes. For me, it was when I was in fifth grade, and our whole family had gathered to celebrate my grandmother's birthday. Even though I didn't want to go, my parents took my brother and me to my uncle's house. I barely nodded my head in greeting to anyone, but my aunts pushed me into a room with my cousins, telling us to play together. For the first time in a long time, I talked with my younger cousin. He showed me a toy his parents had brought him from the United States. It looked like a camera, but when you inserted a disk with colored film on it and looked through the viewfinder, there, before your eyes, appeared photographs of the various national parks in the United States. My cousin told me I could play with it, so I demonstrated how it worked to my younger brother, and we enjoyed playing with it for a while.

Before too long, though, the film disk stopped turning when we clicked the button. I tried to see what might be wrong with it, but oh, what to do! The film disk was crumpled and torn. After wondering for some time how to handle this situation, I quietly went outside and threw the disk away. Then I pretended not to know that it had gone missing.

Naturally, my cousin asked me where the film disk had gone. When I kept telling him that I didn't know, he told his mother, and his mother asked my brother and me if we really didn't know what had happened to it. Strangely enough, though, when she asked me that, I felt a flood of emotions. It was an odd and complex mixture of feelings that is hard to explain: sadness, fear, hatred, jealousy, anger, and a feeling that I had somehow been wronged. I sobbed for some time, overwhelmed with these emotions, and swore to myself that I would never go to my uncle's house again. But then the following year, I had no choice but to let my parents lead me there by the hand.

Looking back on it now, as an adult, I recognize that I must have felt a deep sense of envy toward my cousins. Although this is a common childhood experience, the memory still causes a tinge of heartache as the emotions tied to jealousy are complex and evocative of great pain, sadness, and even some anger.

When I become mindful of feeling jealous of someone, I realize that it is never someone vastly different from me, but always someone I can relate to. For example, we might feel jealous when a co-worker, who entered a company about the same time, is promoted before us. We might feel jealous when our friend, who used to live in the same apartment building, moves to a nice big house because they just inherited money. On the other hand, we rarely feel jealous of people we have no relationship with, like Bill Gates or Elon Musk, regardless of how rich and successful they become.

Jealous emotions may range from simple envy to anger or even violence, depending on their intensity. This often occurs when we concentrate on a narrow aspect of someone's life, like their possessions, skills, or appearance, and overlook the full picture. Although we may covet what they have, that individual may also struggle with depression, loneliness, or anxiety because of what they have or the pressures and expectations associated with it.

If we make good use of jealousy, it can motivate us to work hard and develop our own skills. There is an old saying, "The heaven often blesses those with great potential by providing them with a rival who appears to surpass them." If we resist the temptation to succumb to jealousy and instead use it as motivation to improve ourselves, we may eventually come to the realization that the person who sparked the jealousy was, in fact, the greatest contributor to our success.

Admitting it may be somewhat embarrassing, but my drive to attend an Ivy League school was fueled by the competitive spirit I felt toward my cousins in my youth. I told my family that I was going to the United States for my own studies, but, deep down, I wanted to prove to myself and my extended family that I could succeed in my own way. I am pretty sure that without the experience of jealousy, I would not have been motivated to work as hard. Now that I am older, I want to express my gratitude and apologize to my dear cousins for my jealousy, and at the same time offer a warm hug to the struggling, lonely child inside of me.

Chapter 3

# When Feeling Burned Out and Joyless

# Small but Certain Happiness

"YOLO IS PASSÉ; SBCH IS here." When I had asked people in Seoul what they were interested in these days, this was the reply I received. YOLO, which stands for "you only live once," had led to spending beyond their means, and in the end made life more difficult. Hence people were now turning to the idea of finding SBCH, which stands for "small but certain happiness." This phrase was first coined by the Japanese novelist Haruki Murakami in his essay "Afternoon in the Islets of Langerhans."

Murakami described this small but certain happiness with specific examples: "tearing a piece off a loaf of warm, freshly baked bread and popping it into your mouth; listening to Brahms' chamber music while watching the afternoon sun trace shadows through the tree leaves; a drawer full of neatly folded and stacked underwear." People often think of happiness as something that can only be achieved in the distant future, or after accomplishing a grand goal. In contrast, the idea of small but certain happiness suggests that we should look for joy and happiness in little things that we do every day.

I am glad to see that people are now thinking about happiness in a new way. Previously, people tended to regard happiness as the result of many years of hard work. They imagined that it would come only after getting into a good university, finding a high-paying respectable job or buying a dream house. With small but certain happiness, though, it is not just in life-altering fortunate events that we find happiness but also in the present moment as we engage in simple acts of enjoyment.

Put differently, people have come to realize that happiness does not have to depend on many years of struggle and hardship; instead, it comes down to knowing how to appreciate the life that you have been given in this moment. It implies that there can be an infinite amount of happiness outside of the standardized conventions as each individual gets to decide where their own happiness lies. For some, the fragrant smell of freshly made morning coffee is a time of peace and happiness, while for others, it could be the warmth of the sun on their skin, the sight of spring flowers, the feel of a cozy blanket on a chilly day, or simply spending time with their dog or cat after work. In other words, happiness is readily available if we are willing to slow down and pay attention to appreciate what is already in front of us.

Of course, getting married to someone we love, giving birth to a child, and being promoted to a high-level position are all important sources of happiness. The sense of achievement and satisfaction that we feel when we reach these milestones is tremendous. On the other hand, if we think that *only* these milestone events can bring us true happiness, we will end up spending most of our lives chasing after it. And when we achieve one goal, there will always be another one waiting for us. Therefore, it will never be enough, and we will always be busy. To make things worse, if we don't achieve those goals, we may feel that all the effort was meaningless. In contrast, with small but certain happiness, we can feel happiness much more frequently in our everyday lives, even from a gentle spring breeze caressing our skin, for instance.

When I think about the time I have I experienced small but certain happiness, several examples come to mind. First, listening to my favorite music program on Korean public radio is a time of relaxation and happiness for me. I particularly enjoy the *All the Music Around the World* radio program. Whenever it plays a good song that I've never heard before, I feel rich at heart, like one who has accidently stumbled upon hidden treasure.

I also enjoy walking in my neighborhood park every morning. There is a brown bench in this park, where I often sit surrounded by beautiful oak trees. When I sit there for a moment to watch the sunlight sparkling on the leaves and listen to the birds singing, I feel very blessed and content. Whenever I have a lot on my mind, I go to the bench and meditate for a while. I always feel as though my mind has been reset, like a piano that has just been tuned.

Picking out a few new books in a bookshop and leafing through them is also a great source of happiness for me. Books take me on journeys to new worlds that I didn't even know existed. The experience is vicarious, but it broadens my knowledge and deepens my thoughts. Naturally, when I chance upon a good book in my local bookshop, my heart leaps.

Spending time with my close friends is another small but certain happiness. The frank and affectionate meetings with friends who see me not as a Zen teacher or a well-known author, but as a regular human being, give me the solace and strength to remain calm and composed even when faced with the unexpected curveballs of life.

Was it Goethe who said that if you have fresh air, bright sunlight, clear water and the love of your friends, there is no need to be disappointed in life? The older I get, the more those words resonate with me.

*

The fragrance of lilacs tickling my nose as I walk,
the sight of autumn mountains on a clear, dust-free day,
beautiful music I'm hearing for the first time on the radio,
a chair at a bookshop that allows me to sit and read,
a text message from a friend I've been thinking about,
precious free time after finishing work early for the day.
When do you feel such small happiness?

*

When your mind grows tranquil,
you will see things that you haven't noticed before,
both within yourself and in the world.
And then you will feel quite rich already.

*

If you view happiness as a matter of appreciation
rather than ownership, many things you can't own—
such as the sunlight in your room,
the laughter of children, a loving embrace,
the colors of autumn foliage, a stunning sunset,
the soothing sounds of jazz music at night, or
the triumph of your favorite sports team—
can bring happiness into your life.
The important thing is whether you can
slow down and appreciate life.

*

If you are at ease and feeling relaxed,
everyone you encounter on the street
will appear pleasant and lovely to you.
But if you are busy and stressed,
you will see even the most gorgeous person
as little more than an obstacle in your way,
and you will pass them by without noticing.

*

Whatever we focus on,
it will influence the overall state of our mind.
If we focus on spring flowers,
our mind will become bright and beautiful.
But if we dwell on what went wrong,
our mind will grow dark and depressed.
Therefore, we should be careful about
what we choose to pay attention to.

*

One spring afternoon,
I strolled leisurely along a path
with cherry blossoms raining down on me,
while listening to "Shower the People"
by James Taylor. The harmonious
blend of music and cherry blossoms in the air
was simply magical!

*

We can live our lives in two different modes.
One is a life centered on doing,
and the other is a life centered on being.
In a doing-centered life, we feel our life has value
only when we achieve something significant.
But in a being-centered life, we feel our life is
already valuable and even sacred, connected to
the entire universe and the source of love.

*

While the doing-centered life seeks happiness in the distant future,
the being-centered life discovers it in the relaxed feeling of just being.
You find peace, happiness, and love when you seek less
and appreciate what is already here and now.

*

Examine how your body feels as your breath goes in and out.
As you breathe deeply, all tension in your body begins to melt,
leaving you with the feelings of ease, openness, and connection.
Whenever you feel overwhelmed or disconnected,
come back to your breathing and regain composure and focus.

*

If you want something very badly,
the energy of that desire makes you appear tense and desperate.
Leave the outcome to heaven, take a deep breath, and smile.

*

In the world of Zen monks,
one great compliment you can give is:
"That monk, he really rested his mind."
He released everything and realized his true nature.

*

If you look closely at the mind of gratitude,
you will find therein brightness and calm.
If you look closely at brightness and calm,
you will find the qualities of wakefulness and composure.
This is why those who often feel grateful meditate well.

*

If you can control your ambition, you won't overextend yourself.
If you do not overextend, you will not harm your health.
If your health is good, your mind becomes balanced easily.
If your mind is balanced, you will find happiness in little things.

*

If you set material wealth as the final goal of your life,
you may end up with much money but live a lonely existence.
Money needs to flow like a river in order to sparkle.
Otherwise, it begins to foul if it stops moving.
Share it with others and receive more than you gave.

*

Success can be measured not just by how wealthy you are,
but also by the overall quality of your sleep at night.
There is a surprisingly large number of "successful" people
who cannot sleep deeply because their minds remain too anxious.

*

Here are seven tips for better sleep:

1. Have fifteen minutes of worry time.
If you have trouble sleeping because of anxious thoughts,
set aside fifteen minutes every day for deliberate worry.
Write down all your worries and plausible action plans.
Once you finish them, take a few deep breaths and go to sleep.
You no longer have to worry about forgetting your tasks.

2. Find three things you are thankful for.
If you end your day on kind thoughts,
you will feel better and sleep deeper with a warm heart.

3. Read a book or listen to quiet music.
The blue light from smartphones and television screens
inhibits the production of melatonin, the sleep hormone.
Try a book or peaceful music instead.

4. Make your room darker two hours before going to bed.
If you reduce the intensity of your lights two hours before going to bed, your body will prepare itself for sleep.

5. Don't drink alcohol.
If you fall asleep after drinking, you will wake up in the middle of the night and have a hard time falling back into a deep sleep.

6. Take a warm shower ninety minutes before going to bed.
As your warm, relaxed body cools down,
it will be easier for you to fall asleep.

7. Turn down the temperature in your room.
Warm air hinders sleep.

*

It makes a big difference to the body whether
you sleep six hours a night or seven hours a night.
If you sleep one hour less, there is a greater chance of
overeating and depression. You might also have
trouble concentrating and interacting with people.
So you should go to sleep early for tomorrow's sake.

*

For those who don't get enough sleep on weeknights,
sleeping longer at the weekend can help alleviate
some of the sleep deficit. Therefore, give yourself
permission to enjoy a leisurely Saturday morning!

*

Many people mistake excitement for happiness.
Although being excited can be exhilarating,
it is neither sustainable nor peaceful.
Sustainable happiness is anchored in peace.
—Thich Nhat Hanh

*

People with great success often suffer distress and anxiety in order to maintain what they have accomplished. Rather than thinking only about what you may gain, foresee what you may also lose along with your success. Even if you should realize your overflowing ambitions, success can also harm your health, create distance from your family and friends, and take away all your free time.

*

We may be able to love the world, but we cannot own it.
If we look at things on the timescale of the universe,
we humans are only here for a minuscule moment.
Stop exploiting it and start caring for it as a custodian.

*

The world has enough for everyone's need,
but not enough for everyone's greed.
—Mahatma Gandhi

*

If I focus on the things I do not have now,
my life becomes one of lack.
But if I focus on the things I already have,
my life becomes one of gratitude.

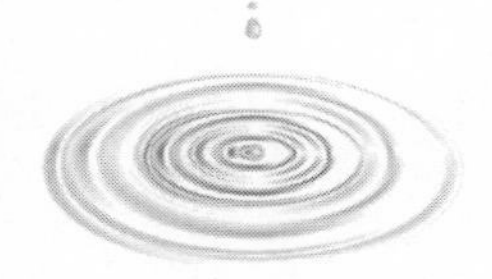

# Where Is Your *Querencia*?

Do you have your very own place of refuge? It is a place where you can be by yourself, catch your breath, and spend a quiet period of healing when life is wearing you down. In Spanish, a place like this, where you can regain your strength, is known as a *querencia*. It refers to the place in a bullfighting arena where the bull goes to rest and recover after fighting a matador. I think that people, too, need a sanctuary of their own where they can rest when they have been wounded and burned out in this battle known as life.

Mihwang Temple, a beautiful Buddhist community at the southernmost point of the Korean peninsula, has become my *querencia*. Not long ago, I finished giving a lecture in the city of Gwangju. Perhaps because of the hot and humid weather in the city, I was getting tired easily and had lost my appetite. When I looked at my itinerary, I was grateful to see that I had a few days of rest scheduled, so I made my way to my place of healing, Mihwang Temple. You need to prepare yourself to travel to there, as it is located at "land's end" in Haenam County and is a long journey. But as laborious as it is to get there, it is also incredibly rewarding.

For starters, Mihwang Temple is so beautiful. The Dharma Mountains, which encircle the temple like a folding screen, amaze everyone who sees their majestic rocky peaks rising into the air like spires. Just looking at the temple's main hall, which is even more elegant and natural for having been stripped of its brightly colored paint over the years, sets the mind at ease. The Buddha that resides within is not overbearing either in size or in appearance, but is as familiar as one of our own ancestors. Around the main hall, blue and purple hydrangeas are in full bloom even during the hot summer, and as you walk further, you can pay your respects to the Buddha's enlightened disciples in the smaller hall.

When people encounter beauty, their preoccupied minds naturally rest and become gentle. Just seeing the resplendent sunsets at Mihwang Temple quietens a noisy mind and lets in the beauty of the setting sun. Imagine sitting on the wooden floor of a temple hall with a close acquaintance and watching the sun slip beneath the line of the ocean, between the islands scattered about in the southern sea. Coming out of the hall after the early morning service to see wreaths of fog climbing up the Dharma Mountains, and the moon so close in the blue sky it looks like it's hanging on the eaves of the hall, is enough to soften even the hardest of hearts and make them wholesome again.

Another reason I like Mihwang Temple is because of the

good people you meet there. The abbot of the temple, Kumgang Sunim, is over fifty but still looks as young as ever. He greets every single visitor with the utmost sincerity, since they have traveled so far to be there; how could one not be moved? He is generous with his time and effort, offering tea and fruit to visitors and listening to their stories, and he has a great sense of humor. Everyone who works at the temple office, perhaps following the abbot's lead, is kind and attentive as well.

During my time resting there, there were four travelers from Europe who had come for a temple-stay program. They were not the type of tourists who come to shop in the department stores of Seoul, but seasoned travelers who had ventured out to a temple at "land's end" to experience the traditional culture of Korea. Maybe this is why our conversations were so interesting and deep. They said they had already visited Ulleung Island, Mokpo and Mount Sokri, which are places popular mostly among Koreans but not as much among foreign visitors. When I asked them how they liked the temple food, they said it was delicious. I suppose that's no surprise: the food is made from fresh vegetables grown by the monks and seaweed that they harvest from the waters near the temple, so the food is not only delicious, it makes you feel healthier just eating it.

When I visited the abbot's room, I saw a painting with his calligraphy that read: "There is a great and gentle hand that protects me." This reminded me that we are not alone here. When things are rough, life may feel lonely and pointless, as if we have been cast into this world on our own, but this is not true. The world is more than just what we can see with our eyes. Although it may be invisible to us, there is a benevolent force, known as the Buddha-nature, love of God, or infinite intelligence and compassion, that surrounds all of us.

When we are completely burned out, however, it can be hard to feel this as we are physically and mentally exhausted. We feel as though we are not in control of our lives, and it is challenging to find motivation and positivity. If you are feeling this way, I recommend taking a short trip to somewhere beautiful, even just for one afternoon. Step away from familiar surroundings and let the new environment stimulate your senses. Spend time in nature, try new foods, and go to interesting shops and museums. If traveling with a loved one, be more spontaneous and use this time to have a heart-to-heart conversation. By taking this time to recharge and reconnect, you can return feeling refreshed and more ready to tackle challenges.

If you ever have the opportunity to go to Mihwang Temple after reading this, you will not regret it. The clear singing of birds and the lively chirping of insects, the refreshing morning air, and the peals of the bell reverberating gently in the temple grounds, will all speed you on your way to healing and self-discovery. As you sip the warm tea given to you by the abbot beneath the beautiful Dharma Mountains, your worries and unease will fade away like the sunset, and you will find your true self once again.

*

Mountains transformed into a sea of light green leaves,
spring flowers blooming on the heels of the cherry blossoms,
the light of the moon and stars in the clear night sky;
if you look around, beauty is everywhere.

*

In a beautiful place,
everything within appears valuable.
When your self-esteem has hit rock bottom,
take the time to seek out a beautiful place
and spend some time there.
You will see yourself differently and
rediscover your own worth and beauty.

*

When we are in pristine and beautiful nature,
our minds instantly relax, and we feel that
everything is delightful and unique, including ourselves.
Perhaps we become aggressive and jaded because
we so rarely experience something pristine and beautiful.

*

Discover a hidden gem in your town.
It could be a cozy alcove in a local cafe,
a peaceful corner beneath a magnificent tall tree,
a comfortable seat in your beloved bookshop, or
a privileged viewing spot of a cherished artwork at a museum.
Visit this place often and take time to reconnect with yourself.

*

The easiest way to beautify your space is to declutter your house.
Throw away the items that you have not touched for a long time,
and make sure the few things that remain are in their proper place.
You can start by removing expired foods, old newspapers, VHS tapes,
battered sneakers, unmatched socks, and random knick-knacks.
This will transform the space into a valuable and beautiful place.

*

Another tip for transforming a space into a valuable place:
don't use several similar items at the same time,
even if you get a new one as a gift.
You don't need to use three different toothpastes at the same time.
Once you finish one, take out a new one from storage.
This will prevent clutter.

*

Wisdom enables us to perceive
simplicity amid complexity.
Beauty enables us to recognize
complexity within simplicity.

*

We human beings desire meaning and purpose in our lives.
True meaning is more easily discovered not through
the pursuit of personal gain, but through serving others.
When our life has been of help to someone, we begin to
feel the meaning and purpose of our own existence.

*

You can find yourself
by losing yourself
in the service of others.
—Herman Harrell Horne

*

My anxiety abates, and my sense of well-being improves
when I release my self-absorbed tendencies
and sincerely concern myself with the welfare of others
by offering support and aid where needed.

*

Everything in this world is interconnected
and interdependent.
Therefore, performing an act of kindness
strengthens that connection,
leading to a feeling of happiness that is our true nature.

*

When times are hard because things aren't going your way,
or you are frustrated because you can't see the solution to a problem,
create some good karma by engaging in a small act of kindness.
For instance, offer nice compliments to people around you,
or make a donation, however small, to a meaningful cause,
or lend help to solve someone else's problem.
Although it may not be directly related to your problems,
amazingly enough, it will help you in some mysterious way.

*

If you wish to be happy, try doing things differently.
On the way home, take a path other than your usual way.
Try ordering a new dish instead of the same old food.
Find a new song to listen to beyond your usual playlist.
Change the location of the furniture in your house.
Try out a book in a genre you don't normally read,
and buy some fresh flowers to put on the table.
We feel happy when we experience positive newness.

*

Twelve small things that bring me happiness:

1. Saturday morning yoga.
2. Making fresh guacamole.
3. Finding a new, nice cafe.
4. Fresh flowers on my desk.
5. A clean and organized room.
6. Listening to an inspiring talk.
7. A leisurely walk in the forest.
8. Volunteering at a soup kitchen.
9. Talking to my mom on the phone.
10. Cooking dinner with close friends.
11. Enjoying the peace of early morning.
12. Taking a relaxing bath while reading a book.

*

If we equate happiness to “a feeling of pleasure,”
we would spend far too much of our lives not being happy.
They say that the ancient Greeks defined happiness as
“the joy felt when one strives to manifest one’s own potential.”
Are you currently working toward realizing your full potential?
Happiness is found in that journey toward realizing it.

*

If you want to be young at heart, learn something new.
No matter how old you are, if you become a student,
you will experience many sparks of joy from learning
and feel young at heart. You will also discover how to
become happy without having to rely on others.

✳

Learning leads to growth.
Growth brings happiness.

✳

One who knows how to enjoy time by themselves,
without depending on others, is a free person.
Having a lot of time does not in itself make a person free.

✳

If you are struggling in a larger task,
do your best in the small task in front of you.
What you can do right now are small things,
and those small things add up to the larger thing.

*

Your beginnings will seem humble,
so prosperous will your future be.
—Job 8:7

*

The quality of a pizza is determined the moment
you first bite into it. It often has to do with
how well the dough was prepared to create the crust.
Only if it is true to the basics of pizza dough
will the other ingredients shine.
If your business is not doing well,
see if you have overlooked the basics.

*

In our minds, we create a framework
of various "conditions" for us to be happy.
We think that if those conditions are met, we will be finally happy.
But the truth is that you are unhappy because
you have those conditions.
They produce the sense of scarcity in your mind and prevent you from
experiencing all the beauty and happiness in this present moment.

*

We become happy
not because we finally got what we wanted,
but because we finally relax without looking for it.

# Finding Peace in a Restless Mind

I WAS GLAD TO HEAR recently from an old school friend whom I hadn't heard from in quite some time. He told me that he had been lucky enough to have been promoted to partner at his accounting firm. He put it humbly, saying that he had been lucky, but I knew just how hard my friend had worked. He had always been smart and a hard worker, even from a young age, so I thought it was only natural that something good should happen to him at his workplace. When he told me that he wanted to buy me dinner, I gladly accepted, and we arranged to meet up. I wanted to chat with him about old times and congratulate him on his promotion.

We had two bowls of soba noodles and a single plate of kimchi pancakes between us, better than any fancy meal. In the scorching heat of summer, those buckwheat noodles in cold broth, flavored with grated radish and garnished with thinly sliced green onions, could not have tasted any better. The kimchi pancakes also complemented the cold noodles well. Watching my friend savoring his soba was yet another joy. We talked about how we had been doing.

As I listened to my friend, I learned that being promoted to partner was incredibly impressive for an accounting-firm employee in their forties. He told me that the company treated him differently now that he had passed such a difficult hurdle, giving him a company car and his own office. He even had his own secretary. But the expression on my friend's face didn't seem all that happy. He went on to tell me that, after he had become a partner, he learned that there were different levels among the partners, and a newly promoted, low-level partner like himself didn't really have any authority. He would have to be at least two levels higher before he had any real power in the firm. He had thought that all he had to do was become a partner, but beyond that mountain, there was yet another mountain, so he wasn't satisfied with his situation just yet.

After hearing this, I was not sure whether I should congratulate him or console him. But if you think about it, a lot of our lives are just like this. We mistakenly imagine that all our problems will somehow disappear if we achieve a long-sought-after goal and triumphantly enter the new world that lies beyond. However, this is not the case at all. In that world, too, there are new rules, different social hierarchies, and subtle discriminations waiting for us.

---

The same was true for me. At first, I thought that all I had to do was leave the secular world behind, shave my head, and apply myself to spiritual practices. But when I became a novice, after being a postulant for about a year, the next step to becoming a fully ordained monk awaited me. Even after I was fully ordained, I had to undergo training and take various examinations and work tirelessly to go from fourth rank to first rank. I experienced similar emotions as a student, too. I thought that if I could just study at Harvard, I would be so happy. But once I was there, I realized that undergraduates, law students, and those studying for MBAs received more respect and better treatment than graduate students in the divinity school, like me. In other words, just because you enter the world that you have been dreaming of, it doesn't mean that your journey ends there and you live happily ever after.

I am not saying that we shouldn't achieve one goal and then work diligently to achieve the next one. We should. However, we must be cautious of equating happiness exclusively with the feeling of excitement that comes with accomplishing something significant. If we do, what happens to the countless days and nights we spend pursuing those goals? Are we meant to feel only average during the day-to-day? Additionally, this mindset only serves us well if the excitement of reaching a major goal continues for an extended period of time. But as we all know, it doesn't continue for very long at all. We immediately begin to see new goals that are even bigger and better, and we run toward those new goals often without a moment of rest.

THERE IS AN IMPORTANT DISCOVERY to be made here: if our ultimate goal is happiness, we won't experience it as long as our mind remains restless while constantly seeking something else. When the mind stops trying to find happiness elsewhere and relaxes in the present moment, we often experience what we have been searching for.

For example, when we purchase a house, a car, or a handbag that we have always wanted, it may seem that those external objects have made us happy. However, if we look deeper, we discover that it was not those objects themselves that made us happy, but the restful condition of our mind, which has temporarily paused the activity of seeking objects. If it were those objects that granted us happiness and peace, then we would remain happy and peaceful for as long as we possess those objects. But the fact is that we aren't, and that we soon start to seek other objects.

Therefore, rather than struggling ceaselessly to find those brief moments of respite, perhaps the quicker way to happiness and peace is learning how to relax our mind in the present moment and appreciate what we already have. Instead of living our lives under the premise that we must wait until we accomplish something big to be happy, we can practice gratitude now and become mindful of how blessed we are already. We can wait our whole lives for that perfect happy moment to arrive, or we can put our seeking mind to rest and discover that it is closer than we might have imagined.

## Chapter 4

# When Loneliness Visits

# Why Are We Lonely?

Why do people feel loneliness? It's not as if there is no one else around us—many of us live with our parents, spouses, or children, and even those who live on their own still have work colleagues whom they see every day and friends with whom they communicate. But even when we live among others, we are still lonely. Having money, power, and fame does not mean that people are insulated from the feeling of loneliness, either. In fact, the more a person has to lose, the more they are on their guard when others draw close, and the lonelier they can be. The Korean poet Sihwa Ryu once wrote: "Even when you are next to me, I still miss you." It expresses the sentiment that even if we have others by our side, we can still feel loneliness. Why is that?

The American psychologist Carl Rogers, the founder of person-centered therapy, explained the reason why we human beings are so lonely. He said we are afraid that if we show other people who we really are, they might judge us or even reject us for our shortcomings instead of warmly accepting us. Although we want to have deeper connections with people by opening up and showing our true selves, there is no guarantee that they will support us. There is also a risk that they might even go around spreading our secrets to others. Therefore, we feel hesitant about letting people really see us, and continue to wear social masks. By hiding our true selves and interacting with people on a safe and superficial level, we do not risk being criticized or hurt by them. However, this also means that we cannot make any deep and meaningful bonds in such meetings, so we are often left with the feeling of loneliness in our hearts.

It is understandable that we cannot easily reveal our true selves at school or work, but why are we often unable to show our true selves to our family members, of all people? Why are there psychological barriers between parents and children, between siblings and between spouses? According to Carl Rogers, psychological barriers are first created inside children when their parents do not treat them with unconditional acceptance and positive regard in a safe environment. If those parents themselves never really had the experience of being respected by their own parents, they are more likely to judge and control their children's thoughts and behaviors in the same way they were treated as children. To give one example, if a parent only recognizes and praises a child when that child acts in the way the parent wants, that child will begin to pay less and less attention to their own feelings and look more to the parent's wishes and instructions. Children raised in this sort of environment find it difficult to freely express their true emotions in front of their parents and routinely suppress them instead. They become accustomed to hiding their feelings and acting as if nothing is wrong.

It can be similar with siblings and spouses. Since family members are close, we may think that there is no need to practice good manners, or that we already know everything about them. Hence, we don't feel much need to listen to them. As we become adults, we also spend less time with our family and more time with our friends at school or our colleagues at work. We gradually have fewer shared experiences and can end up living in different worlds. For these reasons, many of us find it easier to open up to friends than we do to our own family. Nevertheless, we still hope that when we reveal our true and unvarnished selves, our family will be on our side, understanding how we feel and accepting us warmly just as we are. But unfortunately, that doesn't always happen.

WHAT WOULD HAPPEN IF OUR family did not judge us but instead accepted us truly? Then there would be no reason for us to hide our thoughts and emotions behind a mask, and we could express ourselves without fear. Children who grow up in such an atmosphere will have an easier time realizing their potential and blossoming in life. They will affirm their own choices and not be easily led by the opinions of others. Even if they fail, they will accept the responsibility for that failure and, after some time has passed, they will recover. They will also tend to respect others and act with consideration toward them.

This is because those who have experienced respect know how to respect others.

Of course, not all of us have had parents or siblings who accepted us for who we were when we were growing up. That does not mean we have been doomed for life, as it is never too late to form good relationships with people who accept and support us. Maybe it is someone a little further along than us on the road of life, or a loving friend who has been on our side. If there is absolutely no one like that in your life, you can look for a good psychotherapist or counselor who is right for you. With their acceptance and support, you can grow to become less concerned about other people's opinions and more comfortable with yourself.

All of us feel lonely sometimes, especially when we cannot share what is truly going on inside with others. If someone close to you tries to open the door of their heart and share what is really going on, I hope that you will suspend your judgment and listen attentively and warmly. And if you can also open your own heart a little bit more and let them really see you, they will open their door even wider, and you will be able to develop a deeper and more meaningful relationship.

*

We human beings play multiple roles in life;
you can be a parent, a spouse, a daughter, a sister, a niece, a friend,
a boss, a coworker, a customer, a teacher, a student, a neighbor, etc.
But what we know about a person is only one or two of those roles.
So even if you think you know a person well,
in truth you only know a small part of that person.

*

The reason we have difficulties in our relationships
is that we don't have much desire to understand the other person,
while having a far greater need for them to understand us.
So we tell the other person to listen to us for a moment,
with neither of us actually listening to the other,
but instead each trying to say what we want to say.
As a result, we raise our voices and grow further apart.

*

I said that I was lonely.
He replied that everyone is lonely.
That was not the response I was hoping for.
Now I am even lonelier than I was before.

*

When they empathize with me
and truly listen to what I have to say,
I feel a deep connection with them.
However, if they continue to repeat their own views
without attempting to understand my perspective,
even after many hours of conversation,
I become emotionally drained and feel lonely.

*

If there is one person in this world who accepts you just as you are,
you can maintain your sanity and find courage to go on.
If you are struggling because you have not yet met such a person,
then seek out a psychotherapist who is a good fit for you.
Friends may cut you off when you speak, but a good therapist
will listen closely with a receptive mind until you are finished.

*

When our body is unwell, we see a doctor without resistance.
Yet if our mind is unwell, we resist seeing a specialist,
thinking that we can somehow snap out of it.
It can make the condition much worse than it needs to be.

*

Suspicious people find it hard to trust others,
and, therefore, remain isolated and alone.
Conceited people find it hard to mingle with "average" people,
and, therefore, remain isolated and alone.

*

The reason we are lonely is not that
there are no people around us,
but because our hearts are closed to them.
Have the courage to open up and speak to them first.
You will be surprised to discover
how many things you have in common.

*

If parents have self-respect and a sense of humor
even in difficult situations,
their children can have high self-esteem and grow into happy adults.
On the other hand, if parents are ashamed of their children
regardless of their financial situation or
the quality of education they provide,
the children may face psychological problems when they grow up.

*

Each of us in our lives is creating a unique version of our own dance.
Failure, disappointment, and hurt are part of that dance, too.
If parents try to dance for their child to spare them pain,
at some point, the child has to learn to dance that part on their own.
Remember that it is your child's dance, not your own.

*

Our intentions may be pure and worthy,
but we may still do more harm than good to others.
This is due to the misconception
that what has been good for us must be good for others.
So before you do something for someone else,
ask yourself whether they really want it.
Doing something for someone else that they don't want
will do more harm than good.

*

It is not good if you take on excessive responsibility as a parent
and try to solve your grown children's problems.
It is equally not good if you have excessive guilt and
blame yourself for all your children's problems.
We should not, and indeed cannot, be responsible for
someone else's life, even if they are our own children.

*

If you find yourself pleading with a parent
who seemingly favored your siblings over you,
hoping for more love and attention,
they will likely make excuses and remain unchanged.
Resist the urge to change your parent as it may hurt you more.

*

When we understand our parents not as our parents
but as people who can make mistakes,
only then do we become adults.

*

People behave strangely all of a sudden
when they feel anxious and afraid.
If someone you know is acting out of character,
see if you have unknowingly provoked anxiety and fear in them.

*

There is a difference between loneliness and solitude.
Loneliness is being by yourself and yet needing someone,
while solitude is being by yourself and yet feeling serene.
The situation is the same, but depending on the state of mind,
you can feel hopelessly lonely or perfectly content and free.

*

Loneliness is the poverty of self;
Solitude is the richness of self.
—May Sarton

*

You can be alone and enjoy the freedom of mind.
But if you begin to dislike being alone
and feel the need to be with someone,
then it instantly changes to the state of loneliness.

*

Being alone has numerous advantages.
We can increase our productivity
and focus on our personal development.
We have the opportunity to tune in to our inner thoughts
and make crucial decisions without the sway of outside opinions.
We can indulge in activities that bring us joy rather than
conforming to the desires of others.
Lastly, being alone reinforces our independence
and eliminates the need to make excuses to anyone.

*

The greatest thing in the world is
to know how to belong to oneself.
—Michel de Montaigne

*

We often interpret being bored as being lonely.
If we interpret it from a different perspective, though,
being bored is free time filled with countless possibilities.
Just because you have nothing to do, don't call yourself lonely.

*

Our distress does not come from the given reality.
Instead, it comes from our mind's interpretation of it.
The reality is, as it were, raw data, while it is the mind's job
to give it meaning. Hence, depending on your interpretation,
the same reality can be felt in wildly different ways.
If you can, interpret it in a way that can benefit you.

*

Although we cannot change events that have already happened,
we possess the power to control our interpretation of them
and how we choose to react to them.
We can consider the unhappy incident
to be the turning point that we have been waiting for
to transform our lives for the better.

*

I often say to myself:
"It could have been worse.
Fortunately, it was not that bad.
I am thankful it was not that bad.
For my own sake, I won't resent others.
I will live the rest of my life gratefully."

*

There are numerous ways in which
God can make us lonely
and lead us back to ourselves.
—Hermann Hesse

# A New Era of "Alone Together"

I DON'T KNOW ABOUT YOU, but I prefer communication through text messages to talking on the telephone. I thought about why this is the case. I think it is because texting is not only convenient but also less intrusive. When my phone rings, I am forced to halt whatever I am doing at that moment to answer it. If I am having a conversation with someone else, I have to apologize and cut that conversation short. If I am eating, I have to put my spoon down and get up from the dining table in order to pick up the phone. And the sounds of a phone ringing can annoy others, especially in quiet places like a bus, theater, library, or class. There is also the added inconvenience of having to go somewhere else to talk in private if you are in a public space.

With texting, however, I can check my messages and reply to them quietly when I have a moment. I don't have to immediately change my situation or my schedule to fit in with that of my interlocutor. It is also easier to be brief and to the point with a text, which means you can save time for the greetings that must be exchanged when talking on the phone. You can also send the same message to a number of people at the same time through a group chat, rather than having to call each person individually and relay the same message. This type of text communication has become much more natural and prevalent with the development of smartphone applications, so texting has taken its place as the natural method of communication for most people in their everyday lives.

On the other hand, just because this text-based conversation is more convenient, and everyone is doing it, does that really mean that it is better? We stare at our phones and frequently exchange text messages with others, but strangely enough we still feel lonely. We can enter the world of the Internet and connect with anyone we know at any time, regardless of where we are, virtually for free. But somehow there seem to be even more people suffering from alienation and loneliness nowadays. What on earth could have led to such an ironic situation?

SHERRY TURKLE, A SOCIAL PSYCHOLOGIST at MIT, calls our current condition being "alone together." That is, we may share the same space, but our minds have gone to different places through different smartphone apps. We often see our children in the same room as us while staring at their own phone, playing a game, sending texts to other friends or becoming absorbed in social media, rather than interacting face-to-face. The same is also true for adults. When we have a meeting at our workplaces, or get together with our friends over a meal, if there is even a single dull moment, we pull out our phones to check new messages or different apps.

Professor Turkle asserts that this connection via the Internet is different from "communication" in the true sense of the word. If either party in a texting conversation feels uncomfortable, they can leave that conversation at any time without having to excuse themselves, which makes it significantly different from a real conversation, where such a thing is impossible. For example, in a real conversation, if I say something and hurt the other person, even if by mistake, I can see that person's reaction and understand how hurt they might feel based on their facial expression or tone of voice. In a text conversation, though, it is not as easy to perceive the other person's pain since their expressions and tone of voice are not visible. Even if I have severely distressed them, I have no way of knowing how much I have hurt them. On top of that, if I get annoyed by or uncomfortable with someone, I can simply block the conversation.

Another new phenomenon brought on by the use of smartphones is that we can become uncomfortable and even anxious if we spend time on our own without our phones. We feel as vulnerable as if we have come out of the house without wearing trousers. As we get into the habit of constantly checking text messages or other people's lives on different social media, we don't want to be left alone without the Internet connection. If we text a friend and they don't reply for a while, it feels like they are ignoring us, or even like they have abandoned us, and it becomes more and more difficult to bear spending time alone.

I ASKED MY FRIEND MISUK Ko, who is a well-known cultural critic in South Korea, why many people find talking on the phone or meeting in person a bit of burden, even though many of us feel lonely. She answered that it is because people want to connect with others and yet they don't want to feel discomfort or inconvenience. For instance, in order to meet with someone face-to-face, we first need to arrange a time and place to meet, then we need to get ready before going out to meet them, pay the cost of a meal or a cup of coffee there, and listen to the other person talk for some time. If we think about it, the whole process requires quite a bit of effort. Since we don't want to spend this amount of time and energy, we opt out of a meeting and use our easy smartphone to keep in touch instead. Another good example is breaking up with someone via text message. If you do it over a few text messages, it is convenient and safe as you don't have to see them get disappointed or angry. Thus, you yourself don't get as hurt and feel protected.

However, according to my friend, this method of communication robs us of the opportunity to experience what is beautiful and good about face-to-face communication. The feeling that we are in this together, the bond that we feel as we get to know the other person deeply, the joy that we have for being understood and respected, the amazing experience of witnessing vulnerability and reconciliation, the sharing of private stories or important information that we don't normally tell to other people—all of these things are only possible if we meet someone face-to-face.

IN THE END, IF WE really want to overcome the new loneliness, I think we have to be willing to experience some inconveniences and have more face-to-face meetings. For instance, why not actually arrange to meet up with your friend to whom you've said, "Hey, we should meet up sometime." In addition, we can also practice "smartphone detox" once a while by savoring time spent by ourselves, whether reading a book, taking a walk, or meditating at home. When we are comfortable in our own company as well as in the company of others, we can find peace and contentment no matter what situation we are in.

*

When I was young, we used to hide our diaries away
in a locked drawer so that others would not see them.
However, it is now ironic that we openly share
every detail of our daily lives through social media.

*

Social media is created to connect people.
Yet people feel more isolated and disconnected
from the real world than ever before. Isn't it ironic?

*

I reconnected with an old friend, and we met over dinner.
However, my friend brought along a companion—his smartphone.
During our conversation, he divided his attention
between me and his companion, unable to fully focus on me.

*

After the advent of smartphones,
we long to be closer but being close feels a bit burdensome.
Do you sometimes feel this way, too?

*

We exchange text messages with friends
living thousands of miles away,
but we fail to communicate with our neighbors
who are standing outside.
We connect with individuals online who hold similar political views,
yet it is challenging to find someone with whom we can share
our everyday emotions. This is the era in which we live.

✳

If it is not something that you can say face-to-face to someone,
we ought to think twice about posting it on social media.
A carelessly tossed-out criticism can hurt someone gravely.

✳

I once posted on social media a nice photo
I had taken while hiking in Canada.
After seeing the photo, everyone went on
about how jealous they were.
What that photo didn't show, though, was
just how many photos I had to delete,
how desperately I had to fight off the flies
to get to that scenic spot, and just how
hungry and tired I was while taking that photo.

*

Which would you rather have?
A thousand new followers,
or one new genuine friend?

*

Perhaps we are lonely because we expect too much from a single friend. This friend must be honest, caring, loyal, intelligent, and trustworthy. They must have similar hobbies, living standards, and political views. No wonder we feel lonely. If there is one area in which this friend is a good fit for us, we should meet that friend and share the same area of interest. If we look for friends who suit us in all areas, we may remain lonely for a long time.

*

When I think carefully about my life, it seems that
my best friend changes about once every seven to ten years.
If you have grown apart from a friend
and are feeling lonely—maybe because they have moved,
got married, switched jobs, or just become so busy that they don't
have time to see you—wait a bit.
The universe will send you a new best friend if you ask for them.

*

A reporter who has met a lot of successful people once told me,
"The thing about successful people is that no matter
how many other people they meet, they never get tired."
New opportunities and ideas are discovered when talking to people.

*

If you really want to improve your life,
don't wait passively for someone to come and change it.
Instead, actively look for people who can guide you.
When you make the first move, the universe will respond.
If you don't knock on the door, it will stay closed.

*

We don't get to know people when they come to us;
we must go to them to find out what they are like.
—Johann Wolfgang von Goethe

*

It's not that they are a bad person,
it's just that they are not a good fit for you.
Even a good person, if they are not a good fit,
in the end can become a bad person to you.

*

It is hard to work with someone
whose personality is the opposite of yours.
Instead of attempting to change your personality
and befriend them, focus on building trust first
through the quality of your work.
It may take time, but once you have built up that trust,
working together will become much easier.

*

When we are with others, we want to be alone.
But when we are alone, we want to be with someone.
Then perhaps our problem is not in being alone,
nor is it that there are too many people around us,
but in our habit of going back and forth,
not wanting to be alone when we are alone,
and being uncomfortable when we are with others.

*

Do you have these thoughts when you go to a spa?
When you go into the hot tub, you wish it were two degrees cooler.
When you go into the cool tub, you wish it were two degrees warmer.

*

The fundamental cause of loneliness is not being alone.
If that were true, then we would always feel lonely when we are alone.
However, there are moments when we feel free and at ease
even when we are by ourselves.

*

Loneliness adds beauty to life.
It puts a special burn on sunsets and
makes night air smell better.*
—Henry Rollins

*

Until you come to the realization of who you truly are,
no matter how good your relationships and circumstances are,
you will be unable to shake off the feeling that you lack something,
a feeling of subtle emptiness and longing in your heart.
This is because living without the true knowledge of who you are
leads to the illusion that you exist separately and independently
from the rest of the universe. Until you can sense that you are
the entire universe, nothing will satisfy you completely.

# Seeing Loneliness as It Is

NOT TOO LONG AGO, I had a sudden feeling of loneliness on a Saturday afternoon. I had a day off and the weather was nice, but I had no one to meet and nobody got in touch with me. Usually, when I have a gap in my busy schedule like this, I enjoy my time alone and spend it reading or exercising, but that day was a little strange. Admittedly, I could have alleviated my loneliness by reaching out to friends and asking them to have lunch with me. But on that day, I was not in the mood for it. I wanted to delve deeper into the feeling of loneliness, understand its root causes, and explore effective ways of overcoming it.

TO START, I WONDERED ABOUT the fundamental cause of loneliness. People generally say that they are lonely because they have no one at their side. That is, the reason they are lonely is that they are alone. But if you think about it carefully, this cannot be the ultimate cause. People can feel isolated even when surrounded by friends and family, so I don't think we stop being lonely just because we are with someone.

Another reason why being alone may not be the fundamental cause of loneliness is that, if it were, then the time we spend alone would always be accompanied by the pain of loneliness. But that is not in fact true. Speaking for myself, I often feel that time alone is a gift. Others, too, tell me that when they are alone, they feel light-hearted, free and easy, as they don't have to worry about what other people think or want. In the end, it is difficult to say that the cause of loneliness is simply being alone.

What, then, could the cause be? As I continued to examine my own mind, I came to a small realization: the feeling of loneliness arose when I had the thought that I needed to meet someone to feel better. Before having that thought, I was quite all right. But once that thought arose in my mind, I immediately felt a sense of lack and developed a kind of mental resistance to being alone. And interestingly, whenever that feeling of resistance emerged, I felt quite lonely. This led me to think that loneliness might be just a form of mental resistance to the present situation.

On another occasion, I had a different realization. I noticed that my mind was interpreting being idle and bored as being lonely. To escape my inner boredom, I wanted to do something with someone. As soon as I had that thought in my mind, I turned time spent alone into something difficult that must be avoided.

In other words, the feeling of loneliness arose not necessarily from the external situation of being alone but from the internal thought about being alone. It was my interpretation that was causing me to feel lonely.

If we feel lonely in spite of being with someone, however, the cause of that loneliness can be different. We generally feel lonely in these situations if we sense that no one there is on our side, or that no one is trying to understand us. When we feel that we do not belong to the place, regardless of how many people there are, we feel isolated. In short, it is the absence of connection that causes people to feel lonely. Then the question remains: how can we restore this sense of connection?

The most basic way to do this is to show others your genuine self. Everyone wears a social mask that is suited to the role they play. You might play the role of the boss at work, for example, and then when you come home, you might play the role of mom or dad, wife or husband, daughter-in-law, son-in-law, daughter or son. In order to play these roles properly, we have no choice but to show only the part of ourselves that is appropriate for that situation and for the person we are with. But if you want to form a deep and genuine relationship, you must occasionally show your other sides, such as your vulnerability, weakness, playfulness, innocence, and humor. Then the other person will show you the genuine self that they had hidden behind their role. Naturally the two of you will feel a deeper connection and grow much closer.

If you feel lonely because there is absolutely no one around to spend time with, you should look out for opportunities to meet people. I would recommend attending a meet-up of some kind—perhaps a reading group, a hiking group, a spiritual group, a knitting group or a dance group—that both suits your interest and will help you grow in some meaningful area of yourself. Those who are older could also check out a local senior community center, if there is one. If you put in a little bit of effort and overcome the initial discomfort, you will soon meet people you would like to spend time with.

Lastly, I would also recommend looking at the numbers saved in your phone contacts and reaching out to friends you have not heard from in a while. I believe that we are lonely not because we have no friends, but because we do not reach out first. Do not forget that you have to take the first step, and then the world will come to you.

## Chapter 5

# When Facing Uncertainty

# The Courage to Say "I Can't"

I WAS MOVED RECENTLY BY a recitation of "Courage," a poem written by the Korean poet Lee Kyu-gyeong. It fittingly starts with the inspiring line "You can certainly do it."

You can certainly do it.
That's what people said.

You must work up your courage.
That's what people said.

So I did.
I worked up my courage.

I worked up my courage and
I said:
I can't do it.

The poem has a surprising twist. I thought for sure that the first line would be followed by verses endorsing the values of the industrial age, such as "I will work hard, work up my courage, and succeed without fail," but instead it ended with a frank personal confession: "I can't do it." It seemed as if the poet was saying that shedding blood, sweat, and tears to succeed is not the only kind of courage; acknowledging one's limitations, admitting "I can't do it," and recognizing that a certain path may not be right for them, also takes courage.

When I think about it now, the seven years I spent in the United States teaching Religious Studies as a professor was not so much a deliberate choice based on my personal desires, but rather an unconscious choice to follow the path people expected me to take. When I was studying in graduate school, all I could see were those who had graduated before me and gone off to become professors. I didn't even know exactly what it meant to be a professor. I just wanted to be recognized by my colleagues and my own advisers. And so before I knew it, I was walking that path as well. At this important moment that would decide my future, I did not ask myself what I wanted, but instead glanced sideways to see what others were doing and followed them.

Yet once I actually became a professor, I found that it was very different from how I had thought it would be. In the world of academia, teaching my students well was not the most important thing. Writing as many academic articles as possible, obtaining research grants from outside institutions, and producing works that would please my senior colleagues were the ways to gain recognition and promotion. More than anything else, though, everyone was so incredibly busy. Traveling to conferences around the world to present new papers and network with other scholars was also important. Hence, the more successful a professor was, the more time they spent away from the university.

As I entered my fourth year as a professor, I couldn't ignore the truth any longer: I just did not have what it took to become an outstanding scholar. I wrote academic articles, but spent far too long over them. My shy and introverted nature prevented me from being proactive in securing research grants and effectively networking with other scholars. Moreover, I had initially studied religion because I wanted to walk the path of spiritual awakening like the Buddha, not because I wanted to write excellent academic articles. I gradually lost interest in the scholar's life.

One of the most important factors in happiness is the level of control we have over the direction of our lives. Participating in activities that align with our individual desires and needs, as opposed to conforming to external expectations, instills us with a heightened sense of ownership and direction, resulting in a happier existence. Even if an activity is widely considered pleasurable, if we lack control over it, it can still make it feel like a struggle for us. Unfortunately, many people find themselves in this situation, as they lack the courage to say "I can't do it" or "This is not the right path for me." Instead, they follow the expectations set by those around them, rather than charting their own course.

According to the psychologist Taekyun Hur, it is important

to learn how to give up in order to be happy. Giving up does not mean being passive; it means allowing yourself to discover a new path. When I started talking about giving up my job as a professor and returning to Seoul to open a nonprofit organization called the School for Broken Hearts, most people around me expressed concern and tried to dissuade me. To be frank, I, too, was not entirely sure about it at first. I was worried about whether enough people would be interested in our programs and enroll; I didn't know if I would enjoy teaching adults instead of college students. But now, not yet five years later, there is a second branch of the School for Broken Hearts in the city of Busan, and they have become a meaningful place where I and fifty other instructors lead over 3,000 students a year through lessons of healing and growth.

Every now and then, after I give a talk, students approach me with tears in their eyes, expressing their disappointment at failing their qualifying exams once more and their uncertainty about what to do next. After offering a warm, supportive hug and acknowledging their feelings, I usually offer this advice:

It's okay to say "I can't do it." Maybe this path is not the right one for you. If you stop following what other people are doing and start asking yourself what the right path is for you, you can become much happier than if you had passed that exam. If you look back ten or twenty years from today, you might even say that failing the exam was the best thing that ever happened to you. It was a blessing in disguise! So even if you feel at a loss right now, work up the courage to explore your own path.

*

When life gets busier and harder,
give yourself the special gift of pausing.
Stop what you are doing for a moment,
close your eyes and take a step back.
As if you are looking at yourself in a mirror,
examine how your body is feeling
and what your mind is telling you now.

*

When your mind has become calm,
use the power of that calmness to examine
whether you really must continue what you are doing,
which way is the right direction for you,
and what it is that you really want from this life.
The wisdom in that calmness will give you the answers.

*

When things do not go our way,
we pause for a moment and reflect inwardly.
With the new insight from the pause,
we try again with renewed determination
in a more promising direction.
That is why failure often serves as
the foundation for future success.

*

Just because something you desired did not happen,
it does not mean that the effort you put in was meaningless.
The experience and knowledge you gained through the process
will be useful to you in other ways, even if you failed.
If these words do not resonate with you at this very moment,
the day will come when you will be thankful for that experience.

*

Gather your courage and keep moving forward.
Mistakes, failure, and uncertainty are all threads in the tapestry of life.
If you feel sad about falling short of your potential,
use that feeling as a motivation to aim higher and
to explore new possibilities.
Success is not a destination but a continuous process of
learning, adapting, connecting, and evolving.
Trust your instincts to achieve greatness and
don't settle for mediocrity.

*

Becoming too attached to one goal or one person
may lead us to think *only* that goal or that person is right for us.
Try to avoid getting stuck in this limiting mindset;
we live in a world with multiple possibilities to choose from.
When a goal does not work out, we can always set a new one.
When a person does not like us, we can look for someone else.

*

If something is not working out, do not hold on to it for too long
just because you have already invested a lot of time and effort.
Knowing the right time to give up is a form of wisdom.
Giving up does not mean the end, but the beginning of a new path.

*

If you are too obsessed with being perfect,
you will never be able to start.
If you don't start, the task will seem
increasingly insurmountable.
Take the first step and relax.
You can improve it as you progress.

*

If you do not know what you like,
you will desire what others desire.
Since you have no standards, you will have
no choice but to pursue what everyone wants.
Unfortunately, such desires are often expensive,
or there is a lot of competition for them.

*

We forfeit three-fourths of ourselves
in order to be like other people.
—Arthur Schopenhauer

*

Instead of following the crowd
and competing with others to do a task better,
why not take the time to discover what truly suits you
and what fewer people are pursuing?

*

Even with extensive introspection,
it can still be hard to identify your true passions.
Often, greater clarity arises during the process of
taking on new challenges and talking to new people.

*

If it is not something that you are truly pleased with,
take your time and wait a while.
If you search in earnest while waiting,
the right person, the right job, or the right situation
will appear eventually.

*

Don't feel anxious just because your future seems uncertain.
You can only see the road ahead of you one bit at a time,
not the entire road all at once. Likewise,
you can only dream about your future one bit at a time.
Unexpected opportunities will be revealed to you
as you continue to walk the road.

*

I so badly wanted to achieve enlightenment,
and so, without any concern for what others might think,
I shaved my hair and became a monk.
If there is something you really want to do, do it.
In the end, your parents, friends, and the rest of the world
will be happy that you are happy. Have courage!

*

If there is a goal you want to achieve,
write it down on a piece of paper
and then, directly beneath that,
break down your goal into actionable steps.
If you attach that piece of paper to a wall and
look at it for a minute each day,
you will be more likely to put it into action.

*

It is easy to feel depressed when there is a great distance
between who you are today and who you want to become.
Assess your abilities honestly as they are now
and set yourself new and achievable goals.
Every time you accomplish one of those goals,
it will be easier to achieve a slightly bigger goal.

*

We usually want to accomplish many things swiftly.
And yet we rarely set goals for ten or twenty years' time.
Don't be discouraged if you don't accomplish your goal quickly.
Those who run with long, steady breaths do great things in the end.

*

Continue doing your work to maintain a livelihood,
but also explore your interests outside of work.
Pursuing both simultaneously can bring a sense of joy
and eventually lead to making a living from your passions.
Don't just contemplate trying something new;
instead take action even with small steps.

*

Do not sit at home when you are feeling blue.
Move your body and walk around in your local park.
Meet a friend and talk about what has been going on lately.
If your body remains stiff and disconnected from the world,
you won't feel much difference, no matter
how much you change your mindset.

*

When I travel, I use a disposable razor.
The blades often grow dull with use,
so every time I shave, I nick myself a little.
But if I slow down and approach the task gently,
I am able to avoid further nicks.
Going slow and gentle is key.
Rushing leads to difficulties.

*

If you feel that life is hard,
so hard that even walking feels tiring and burdensome,
then walk more slowly, taking only half-steps at a time.
As you walk slowly, at a comfortable speed,
you will realize that life has been hard lately
because you were going faster than you could manage.

# The Two Me's Inside of Me

THERE IS A FAMOUS KOREAN song called "A Thorn Bird" that begins with the line, "There are so many me's inside of me that there is no place for you to rest." This song has been covered by many different singers, and every time I hear it, I am struck anew by how well it expresses human psychology. In particular, the idea of many me's inside of me leading to a "darkness I can't help" and a "sadness I can't overcome" really hits home for me. Even if it is not my intention, the multiple me's can clash with each other in my mind, unwittingly hurting other people and leaving me with little peace of mind.

Psychologically speaking, the multiple me's can be grouped into two basic categories. One is the "me of me," the self that I want to be, and the other is the "me of others," the self that family and society expect me to be. If the "me of me" concerns my personal inner desires, the "me of others" is consumed by the expectations, wishes, demands, and responsibilities of those around me, which I have unknowingly internalized.

Everyone has these two kinds of "me" inside of them, but it is not easy to create a healthy harmony between the two. In particular, the younger you are, and the more authoritarian your parents are, the more the "me of others" can overpower the "me of me." When we are children, we learn social rules and etiquette from our parents, and we have no choice but to live under their teachings and control. But if this control is too severe, even once we have grown into adults, we won't be able to hear the voice of the "me of me," and in extreme cases we might feel that we don't even *have* a "me of me."

For example, some people are reluctant to explore their own interests and values even after they became adults. Instead of asking themselves, they ask others what they should be doing. They are afraid of making mistakes, and, therefore, avoid taking the responsibility that comes with making their own decisions. They tend to formulate their own self-identity through others, often introducing themselves as someone's spouse, the son or daughter of a family, or the parent of a child.

When it comes to happiness, they frequently neglect their own needs and put other people's needs first. Instead of doing things that will make themselves happy, they become dependent, and feel happy only when their parent or spouse is happy, or when their child does well in school. Of course, there are advantages to living as the "me of others." Family members and close friends will probably like them a lot and even praise them; few parents would dislike a child who does not disobey them and does exactly as they are told. Few spouses will dislike a spouse who sacrifices their needs and dedicates themselves entirely to their family. But what about when that child grows up and moves away from home, or what if the parents or spouse pass away first? It would be great if such a person could then listen to the voice of the "me of me," but that is not so easy for someone who has lived their whole life without practice.

Most people do ultimately find the "me of me" as they grow older. The late Korean novelist Park Wan-suh wrote in her later years: "Now that I am older, I can wear these loose trousers with an elastic waistband; it's nice to be able to live relaxed and free in the exact way I want to. It's nice not to do the things I don't want to do. In all honesty, I don't want to be young again. How great it is to be able to have the freedom to say 'No' to what I don't want to do! Why would I trade that for youth? If I feel like writing more fiction, then I will write it. But if I don't feel like it, then that's fine, too."

As I am crossing the threshold of my late forties, I realize that I am becoming less conscious of the impression I have on others. I don't care much if people recognize me or not on the streets of Seoul; I visit public baths with a light heart, and I hum and occasionally sing to myself while taking walks. I have become quite good at declining requests for lectures or papers if I have too much on my plate, and I no longer wonder what other people think of me.

That being said, if we completely ignore the "me of others" as we live our lives, our relationships with others may sour needlessly. Therefore, the most desirable way of living seems to be one that achieves a proper balance between the "me of others" and the "me of me." Not living under the thumb of the "me of others," always thinking about what others want, nor chasing only after the "me of me," turning a cold shoulder to our relationships with others, but finding the happy balance between the two is, I believe, the answer to living an enjoyable and happy life.

*

There exists simultaneously in everyone
"the self that doesn't want anyone to know" and
"the self that feels comfortable revealing to others."
Rather than repressing the first self and feeling afraid
and ashamed of your dark side, recognize its existence.
The moment you do, you will be more at ease
and able to integrate all aspects of yourself,
leading to a more fulfilling and authentic life.

*

We are programmed in our youth
with certain ideals about how people ought to live.
These ideals make us feel "not good enough"
as we find it hard to live up to them.
By the same token, we are quick to judge others
who don't live by the same ideals while feeling
somehow morally superior to them.

*

You might be overly conscious of others
because you were often scolded by strict parents,
or frequently judged by those close to you.
But you can't always be worrying about what others think of you.
In all honesty, others aren't really all that concerned about you.
So stop caring about it so much and relax.

*

Although it may be disappointing, the person you thought was
deliberately ignoring you was probably not that interested in you.
It is easy to assume that people are preoccupied with us,
when in reality, this is rarely the case.

*

Tips for an easier and simpler life:

1. Don't ask what others have said about you.
2. Say up front what you like or don't like.
3. Let go of things outside of your control.

*

Don't go out of your way to find out
what others are saying about you.
It will only cause you annoyance and hurt.
Arguing with someone who has already decided to
dislike you will do more damage to you than to them.
Master the art of brushing it off and
keep focusing on the work that matters to you.

*

We are bombarded with negative news daily. However,
it is important to consider how many of these news updates are
truly necessary for our well-being. Remember,
we have a choice not to be aware of every piece of negative news
in the world at all times.

*

Is your belief about yourself holding you back
from achieving your dreams?
If you believe that you are unlovable or incapable,
who planted that belief in you?
Was it always yours? Or did you unwittingly
start to believe what someone said to you?

*

Don't let negative opinions of others dictate your future.
Stand up for yourself and tell them to back off.
You are in the driver's seat of your own life,
and have the power to make them disembark.
Once you have made your position clear, continue
driving along the road you have intended to travel.

*

When people dislike some aspect of themselves,
rather than changing it,
they try to change others who exhibit the same trait.

*

Those who have achieved their dreams or
who have truly risen to a challenge
won't be so quick to tear down the dreams of others.
If you look closely, you'll notice that those without courage
often belittle others and try to bring them down to their level.

*

If you are trembling with fear and thinking, "Can I really do it?
How could someone like me dare to attempt a goal like that?"
Then this is precisely the goal you must go for if you want to grow.
Even if you fail, and things do not work out as you hoped,
you will learn something valuable and grow from that experience.

*

Between "painful things that are familiar"
and "unfamiliar things that can bring happiness,"
People often choose the familiar.
There is no need to be that loyal to your pain.
Even if you are afraid because it is unfamiliar,
have courage and choose the path of happiness.

✳

In any given moment, we have two options:
to step forward into growth,
or to step back into safety.*
—Abraham Maslow

✳

People don't want safety as much as they think they do.
Even those who seek safe jobs or safe relationships
grow bored once they have reached that safe situation.
So, every now and then, rather than always choosing safety,
try something a little difficult or unfamiliar that will lead to growth.

*

The reason people don't succeed
is that they only think inwardly
and never put those thoughts into action.

*

Master Yoda once said,
"Do or do not.
There is no try."

*

When we first discover a problem,
we may feel hesitant to confront it directly.
However, if we continue to delay action, it will only escalate.
Don't wait too long and regret that you didn't deal with it earlier.
If you look closely, you will see a way to solve it.

*

If we do not change ourselves,
the world will see to it that we change.
Of course, the latter is much more painful.
But that pain is there to make us grow,
not necessarily to torment us.

*

At the bottom of the mountain,
we may see the summit clearly.
But once we start climbing the mountain,
the summit will be hidden behind trees.
Likewise, when we set a goal and move toward it,
it will not feel like we are moving forward,
but there is still progress.
Don't be discouraged but press on.

*

Successful people who reach the top through their efforts
do not have a superiority complex, as they are aware of
the help they received along the way.
Those who have had a stroke of luck or who have started
the climb recently often have an air of self-importance,
asking, "Do you know who I am?"

*

The greater a person's success is,
the simpler their business card.

*

When you achieve something remarkable,
you will feel that this is only the beginning.

*

*Advice I would offer to my younger self in my teens:*
Remember that the challenges and embarrassing moments
that seem overwhelming now will appear minor in hindsight.
Don't place too much weight on the opinions of your friends.
There are numerous paths you can take in life,
and if your current plans don't pan out, don't lose hope.
Life has its ups and downs, but it gets better as you grow older.

*Advice I would offer to my younger self in my twenties:*
Take it easy and have confidence that things will work out in the end.
Live true to yourself and let your unique qualities shine,
without feeling the need to measure up to others.
Allow life to unfold naturally and resist the urge to plan everything.
Embrace the unknown and appreciate the journey.

*Advice I would offer to my younger self in my thirties:*
Don't settle for small successes or the comfort of familiar situations.
Continuously seek new knowledge from others by asking questions.
When evaluating people, focus on their character,
life experiences, and sense of humor, rather than
external factors such as appearance, education,
or family background. Stay connected with
nature and reading, and keep your body
active through exercise.

*Advice I would offer to my younger self in my forties:*

Don't get too caught up in your work;
make sure to set aside time for self-care.
Invest in meaningful relationships,
both personal and professional.
Don't be afraid to take calculated risks and
pursue passions besides your work.
Appreciate beauty in every moment.
Travel with your parents while they can.
Remember to give back and help those in need.

*

Instead of being timid and fearful,
aim to become strong and resilient.
Then gain wisdom through life experiences
and put it into virtuous actions,
for achieving personal growth and
making a positive impact in the world.

# Listen First to the Pain Inside of You

When my thoughts dwell on regrettable memories, or anxious worries about the future, I free myself from the grip by shifting my focus to the sensations in my body. By paying attention to how my shoulder, stomach, or chest feels in the present moment, I break away from the mental loop of negative thoughts. This allows me to find peace and relaxation in the present, and I come to understand that it is only my own mind that is causing distress, while the world around me remains undisturbed and peaceful.

This method of focusing on the present moment through mindful awareness of physical sensations was introduced to me through the teachings of Thich Nhat Hanh, a prominent peace activist and Buddhist monk. When Thich Nhat Hanh visited Korea several years back, I was thankfully charged with the task of interpreting his talks. Though he was eighty-eight years old at the time, he taught without missing a single day.

As I watched him, he seemed to me like a peaceful and benevolent pine tree. When I was at his side, my mind was calm and tranquil under the generous shade of his branches. In particular, when he engaged in walking meditation, I could sense that with each step he took, he was fully present in that moment and in that place. It was as if he was showing me that meditation practice is at its heart neither mysterious nor complex, but something familiar and easy to carry out.

Among his many wonderful teachings, I was particularly impressed by the lesson that we can restore our estranged relationships with the practice of mindfulness meditation. When we hear the word "meditation," we may mistakenly think of traveling to a remote mountain monastery and disconnecting from the world in search of a transcendental experience. However, if your mindfulness meditation practice is successful, regardless of where it is performed, you will gradually want to reconnect with the world and repair any relationships that have been put under strain due to arguments or misunderstandings. This desire to restore relationships is a natural outcome as the heart begins to heal with mindfulness meditation.

In his book *Peace Is Every Step,* Thich Nhat Hanh says that while flowers and detritus might seem to be two very different things, existing independently from each other, this is by no means true. In order for flowers to exist, they must receive nutrients from the soil, which come from detritus; after some time passes, flowers, too, will fall to the earth and become detritus. Through the example of flowers and detritus, he teaches us that nothing in this world exists as separate and alone, but that all things rely on each other and exist together as one.

This teaching can be applied to our relationships as well. For example, if someone we love dearly is ill, though we may not become physically ill ourselves, our heart aches for this person and we suffer, too. This truth of our interconnectedness with the world and each other is also a fundamental realization sought by practitioners of meditation in their pursuit of enlightenment. Thus, when we have a falling-out with people close to us, restoring those relationships can bring not only a lot of healing but also the realization of this same fundamental truth.

How, THEN, CAN WE RESTORE these broken relationships? In answer to this question, Thich Nhat Hanh has said that we must first listen to our own suffering. We need to devote our attention to discovering where this suffering is making our bodies tense, and how it is making our hearts ache. If we first shine the light of loving attention on ourselves and become mindful of the pent-up emotional energy in our body and mind, that energy becomes softer and then gradually melts away. Only then will our minds be open to understanding the suffering of others.

The next step is to reach out to those with whom we have had estranged relationships. Try to meet them face-to-face and listen attentively to their stories of suffering. Even if they misunderstand us and lash out at us, or say something that is not true, we must not react defensively or angrily. Instead, we should listen to them patiently until they have shared all their hurt, so that they can also release their pent-up emotions. This only becomes possible when we have first listened to the pain inside of ourselves, and realized that their pain and our pain do not exist independently but are interconnected.

As I interpreted Thich Nhat Hanh's words, I asked myself, "Have I thoroughly listened to the suffering inside of me?" I wondered whether I had tried to avoid my own suffering by staying busy with work, watching movies and talking about other people's problems. People spend a lot more time paying attention to external objects. As such, we are not accustomed to observing the feelings in our bodies and minds carefully. But to be healed, we need to redirect the light of our loving attention toward our inner landscape.

Thich Nhat Hanh has taught: "We were born so that we might wake up from the illusion that we all exist separately." We must not forget that, just as flowers and detritus rely on each other to exist, our own healing and the healing of others are not separate but interconnected.

Chapter 6

# When Enlightenment Has Yet to Occur

# Ways of Living Harmoniously

A FEW YEARS AGO, I entered Bongam Monastery to participate in the autumn meditation retreat. There were over a hundred monks who had come to the monastery to join the retreat. Among these many monks, there were some familiar faces I was glad to see, having lived with them at other monasteries in the past, but I also saw many new faces. Monks are no different from anyone else when it comes to living with strangers. At first, the atmosphere was a bit awkward and even tense. After a while, though, we became quite proficient at carrying out what needed to be done in order for everyone to live together in harmony.

One of the first unspoken guidelines I learned as a young monk from seasoned monastics was this: *Don't insist on doing things in your own way.* When monks from all parts of the country come to live together in one place, you experience some interesting phenomena. For instance, during the morning chanting service, you sometimes hear different speeds and tones when reciting Buddhist scriptures. Monks who have lived at Songgwang Monastery, located in the southwest region of Korea, tend to recite slowly and serenely, while the chanting of monks from Haein Monastery, located in the southeast corner of Korea, tends to be swift and vigorous, much like the vibrant energy of Mount Gaya on which the monastery is located. The style of a monk's recitation is often determined by the home monastery where that monk first received his training.

The problem, though, is that if each monk insists on reciting in his home-monastery way and makes no attempt to harmonize with the other monks, we end up with a discordant, offbeat recitation that is quite painful to listen to. Just because we are familiar with our way of doing things, it doesn't mean that this way is objectively right and others are wrong. When we are living with others, we make an effort to adjust to each other so that we can live in harmony.

ANOTHER IMPORTANT GUIDELINE THAT I have followed is this: *Decide from the very beginning that you will work more.* On the day before the meditation retreat is to begin, everyone gathers to determine their individual duties. There are a wide variety of duties: preparing meals in the monastery kitchen, cleaning the halls and meditation rooms, patrolling the monastery and surrounding mountains, and so on. Some of the duties may be handled by a single person, but in most cases a number of people will carry out these duties together. When many people are working in a group, it is not uncommon for disagreements to break out after a couple of weeks because some people seem not to be working as hard as others.

While each of us is well aware of how hard we ourselves have been working, we don't know how hard others are working as we don't see them all the time. Hence, we may feel that we are working above and beyond while others are not. Of course, it would be ideal if we never thought with such a calculating and discriminating mind in the first place. We suffer mentally if these sorts of divisive thoughts occupy our mind. But should such thoughts arise, if we resolve from the start to work more than others, our minds will be that much more at peace.

ANOTHER GUIDELINE THAT I HAVE followed is this: *Accept the given situation with a positive mind.* Prior to the retreat, lodgings are usually determined based on seniority. The older monks are given single or double rooms, while the rest of the community live in large rooms that hold several people. For this autumn meditation retreat, though, everyone older than me got single or double rooms, and, unfortunately, I was the first to be assigned to a large room. At times like this, if you fret too much, you could end up being dissatisfied for the entire retreat. But if you quickly take your mind off the matter, you can find many good things in what at first might not have seemed so good.

As I thought about it, I was able to find many advantages to staying in a large room with seven other monks. Firstly, if I were in a single room, there might be times when I would be so tired that I would sleep through the sound of the wooden fish bell at 3 a.m. and miss the dawn service. But since I was staying with other monks, I could sleep easy knowing that one of us would turn on the light before the service. Another benefit is that I could quickly learn any announcements, as one of my roommate monks would share the monastery news with the rest of the room. Moreover, our room was always neat and clean, without any clutter, as each of us always stored our personal items in our respective closets after using them. This would have been much harder if the room was occupied solely by myself.

LASTLY, IF I BECAME DISSATISFIED with someone or some new situation during the retreat, I asked myself: *Am I focusing right now on my meditation or not?* When my meditation practice is going well, I am so focused on examining my own mind that I do not involve myself in the affairs of others. When I am unable to concentrate on what I am supposed to be doing, I begin to see faults in others. But I know that the flaws of others are, in a sense, my own flaws, appearing in the mirror of my own mind. If I did not have similar flaws, they would not bother me that much. At times like this, I try to return to the mindset I had when I first resolved to become enlightened, and calmly carry out my work without wavering from it.

*

Living in a community means sharing
both the joys and the challenges, and
growing together through the experience.
—Anonymous

*

In any community, two types of individuals exist:
passive and reactive or proactive and creative.
The former feels that their lives are mainly controlled by external factors,
while the latter understands their power to shape their own thoughts and emotions.
By actively creating a positive mindset, they turn aspirations into reality.

*

Why would I want to ruin my inner peace
by staying angry at those who have wronged me?
Forgiveness is not for them; it is for me.

*

When someone wrongs us, if it is
someone we have liked, we will most likely
understand and forgive them.
But if it is someone we have disliked,
even if they have done the exact same thing,
we are more likely to hold grudges and
cannot forgive them easily.
It is quite strange how our minds work.

*

If you fight hate with hate,
there will be no end to struggle, and the pain will continue.
Only understanding and love can break the chains of hate.
I bow my head to this simple yet deep truth
that is thousands of years old.

*

We usually dislike changing ourselves,
but we have no issue telling others to change for our benefit.
This is why we remain trapped in patterns of
frustration and disappointment.

*

Criticizing others often leads to defensive behavior rather than
fostering change. To effectively bring about transformation,
start by understanding their perspective and
communicate your suggestions for improvement respectfully.
Without respect, advice is unlikely to be accepted.

*

Let me tell you how to ruin a relationship.
First, assert that your expectations are "common sense";
then, use them to judge those who don't align with your views,
and continually nag them to fit your expectations.
You will likely succeed in driving them away.

*

I hope that I will not be so preoccupied with
being right that I fail to see
when my preoccupation is hurting others.

*

If you want to persuade someone to do what you want,
it is no use to explain your position repeatedly.
Instead, find out first what their main concern is,
and then look for a way to satisfy both you and them.
Then tell them why your way will not only help you,
but also resolve their pressing needs right now.

*

If you often feel a sense of superiority,
that is because a deep sense of inferiority
has taken hold inside of you.
Those who like themselves treat others respectfully.

*

People with a big ego often suffer from low self-esteem.
Low self-esteem leads to an increased need for validation and attention,
which can result in an inflated sense of self-importance.

*

Men should be like this, and women should be like that.
Parents should be like this, and students should be like that.
Politicians should be like this, and monks should be like that.
In this way, we do not see them for who they truly are.
Instead, we see if they fit into our idea of who they should be.
If they meet our standards, we say they are excellent.
But if not, we judge them to be problematic human beings.

*

If a monk speaks of goings-on in the world,
people tell him to stay in his mountain monastery
and not to concern himself with the mundane world.
But if he says nothing and remains quiet, then
people call him selfish for ignoring the suffering of the world.
A monk must learn to navigate life between the two.

*

When you leave your home and embrace the monastic way of life,
your aim is to awaken and share your wisdom for the greater good.
It is important to realize that becoming a Buddhist monk or nun is
not a way to escape the world but rather
a path toward a deeper understanding of it.

✳

If you express your anger without any filter,
it will become bad karma and return to you.
If you just suppress your anger and bottle it up,
it will then emerge as an illness in your body.
If you quietly observe the energy of your anger,
it will change shape on its own and disappear.

✳

When your mind is distressed, observe what is causing the distress.
You will see that it originates in and persists through your thoughts.
But a thought is by nature like a brushstroke on water:
it shows itself momentarily and then disappears without a trace.
Hence, there is no need to dwell on distressing thoughts
which will soon naturally fade away, if you let them.

*

If you have a single anxious thought,
mountains of worry and fear will gather like clouds.
But when that anxious thought passes,
the clear blue sky of your mind reveals itself.
We can experience heaven or hell because of a single thought.
So do not hang on to negative thoughts; just let them pass you by.

*

The sky did not originally have a north, south, east, or west.
Through our language, we named and divided it as such.
Similarly, the world was originally one, without division.
But through our words, we have divided it into millions of pieces,
and delude ourselves into thinking that they have all existed
independently.

*

Winds leave no sound after passing through a bamboo grove.
Geese leave no shadow after flying over a cold pond.
Noble men leave no thought in the mind after completing a task.
—Hong Zicheng

*

When we allow ourselves a deep rest,
our minds grow tranquil, as if empty;
When we must work,
that tranquil mind awakens
and gives birth to new thoughts.

*

There is a chair in a large, empty space.
Naturally your eyes are drawn to that chair
while overlooking the large, empty space.
But the chair could not have been there
if there was not a large, empty space.

In the peaceful and empty space of your mind,
a single thought appears.
Naturally you are drawn to that thought
while overlooking the peaceful space of your mind
which gave birth to that thought.

Awakening to the Buddha Mind
does not mean changing bad thoughts to good thoughts.
Instead, it begins by becoming more aware of
the peaceful and empty space of your mind
where thoughts emerge and disappear.

*

If the mind is in the present, thoughts cease
and the mind naturally becomes tranquil.
This tranquility is empty of forms and boundless,
and, therefore, its depth is without end.

*

All thoughts are merely waves, temporary shapes
made out of the deep ocean of the mind;
after their brief appearances, thoughts merge back into
the tranquility of the boundless mind.

*

When we trust that we are the ocean,
we are not afraid of the waves.
—Sayadaw U. Pandita

# Discovering Your True Self

On a warm spring day, I set everything aside and head to my little quiet place. A brief pause of even ten minutes in the hectic modern world can be restorative to both the body and the mind. If we sit quietly and look inward, we can see the continual appearance and disappearance of thoughts and feelings. It is relatively easy to notice the presence of thoughts and feelings, while it is quite hard to recognize the quiet space after the thought or feeling has passed and before the next one has arisen. Until the emergence of a new thought or feeling, there is a tranquil silence that seems to be devoid of anything. Most of us are unaware of that empty space and simply let it pass us by. This is because, unlike thoughts and feelings, tranquil silence is shapeless, so it is impossible to grasp.

Unlike silence, thoughts and feelings have forms, so they can be observed, explained to others, and put down in writing. Since they appear in our mind, we get into the habit of identifying ourselves with these thoughts and feelings, calling them "my thoughts" and "my feelings." We sometimes even cling to them and use them as the defining aspects of ourselves, saying, "This is the kind of person I am," as though we have intentionally chosen those thoughts and feelings to appear. If you believe that the thoughts and feelings in your mind are truly yours, then think about this question: if they are really you, then have you not existed before the appearance of those thoughts and feelings? When those thoughts and feelings disappear, if they were really you, you would disappear along with them—but have you ever experienced the disappearance of yourself?

You existed before the rising of thoughts and feelings, and will continue to exist even after they all disappear. It is because they are not your true self. They are just like evanescent clouds in a big blue empty sky. What, then, is the real "you" that has existed since long before these clouds of thoughts and feelings? This very question has been asked by countless spiritual practitioners in various traditions. Many have spent their entire lives trying to get to the bottom of it and discover what their true self is. I think each person must find the answer to this question through their own experience. But, on the off chance that my words here might lead someone to have their own awakening experience, I would like to offer them, inadequate though they might be.

I WILL DO AWAY WITH theoretical explanations and cut straight to the chase. What existed before thoughts and feelings arise, and what will remain the same after those thoughts and feelings disappear, is your awareness. When no thought or feeling appears in your awareness, you experience it as tranquil silence, much like the state of dreamless sleep. It is formless, empty, transparent, and peaceful. It is also the ground upon which you exist, and out of which all aspects of you are created. If you look closely, you will be able to see that all thoughts and feelings emerge out of your silent awareness, reveal themselves momentarily, and then disappear back into the silence after a time. In other words, your awareness creates all forms, provides room for them to exist, and reabsorbs them when it is time for them to go.

Now, let us take one step further and explore exactly where this tranquil silence is located. First, close your eyes, breathe in deeply, and let your mind settle down. Then, see if you can recognize the quiet space after a thought has passed and right before a new one has arisen. Feel this tranquil silence. When you can sense the silence, ask if this tranquility exists only inside your body, or outside your body as well? Does the tranquility inside the body exist in a different form from the tranquility outside the body, or is it just one seamless tranquility? Put away the conceptual mind that likes to analyze, and instead just feel this tranquil space in your awareness and let the answer arise naturally from it.

Let us go even deeper and examine if we can find the edge of this tranquil silence. Can you reach its edge? Can you find the beginning or the ending of the silence? Is there any limit in this wide-open space of your awareness? Is there any center? Finally, can you sully your tranquil awareness or change its nature permanently? No matter how loud a sound you make, the silence soon recovers and returns unscathed to its original tranquil form, doesn't it? It is completely unbreakable and imperishable as it does not have any form. You can neither lose it nor make it disappear. It is eternally here.

I sincerely hope that you will become aware of this transparent silence in your own awareness. There within, you will also find deep serenity, eternal freedom, a wellspring of creativity, and a warm acceptance.

*

Feel the space between thoughts.
After one thought ends,
but before the next thought begins,
there is a brief opening
into the space of your limitless awareness.

*

When we break free from the entrapment of thoughts
by coming to the present moment through being aware of breath,
the silent awareness, which had been in the background of thoughts,
awakens and starts becoming aware of itself.

*

When thoughts and feelings become quiet for a while,
we start to become aware of the tranquil awareness itself.
As we come to realize that there is no edge to tranquility,
we sense the boundless nature of our naked awareness,
present not only inside us but also outside the world.
This realization is the first important step toward enlightenment.

*

It is through deep, dreamless sleep
that our bodies are healed and our minds are restored.
Hence the tranquil mind without noisy thoughts
does not imply the state of boredom, or meaninglessness.
It actually means perfect rest and peace, healing and rejuvenation,
as well as the birthplace of creativity and boundless freedom.

*

As we grow spiritually,
so does our idea of God or the Buddha.
The depth of our understanding
is directly proportional to
the maturity of our spiritual mind.

*

If you contemplate the deep meanings
behind religious symbols
and have a direct spiritual experience of them,
you will soon come to understand that
there are underlying similarities among
different religions at their core.
Without this experience, however,
you will be bound by the symbols,
seeing only the differences and
denigrating believers of other religions.

*

We are not human beings having a spiritual experience.
We are spiritual beings having a human experience.
—Dr. Wayne W. Dyer

*

At first, I sought you in that holy icon within the temple.
Next, I sought you in spiritual teachers like gurus and masters.
After that, I sought you in the words of the sacred scriptures.
But now I finally feel your presence everywhere.
You have always been with me, like the air.

*

In the end, you will understand that
the answer to the question you so desperately sought
was not to be found in your destination.
When the time comes,
you will be awakened to the knowledge
that you have had it in your pocket the whole time.
You just have to relax and see what you already have.

*

You can't imagine how much
I've looked for a gift for you.
Nothing seemed appropriate.
You don't take gold down into a goldmine, or
a drop of water to the Sea of Oman!
Everything I thought of was like bringing
cumin seed to where cumin comes from . . .
You even have my love and my soul,
so . . . I've brought you a mirror.
Look at yourself, and remember me.
—Rumi

*

Your only sin is
forgetting who you truly are.
You are not a frail and trembling leaf.
You are the whole tree.

*

Enlightenment is realizing the oneness of the world,
not just with your head but with your heart.
The next time you feel joy from making others happy,
take a moment to reflect on whether there is a distinction
between your own joy and theirs.

*

There is a world visible to our eyes
and a world invisible to our eyes.
Becoming spiritual means starting to
be aware of the invisible world.
As you become increasingly aware of
the world beyond what you see,
you will have the surprising realization that
the visible world and the invisible world
are ultimately not two, but one.

*

The truth is often something we have already known.
This is because it is inherent in us,
but when we hear it again, there is a new depth to it.

*

The happiness discovered upon the awakening of intellect is
a feeling of inner wealth, as if great treasures have been found.
We quickly gain the confidence to establish our own standards
and are not easily swayed by others' opinions.
The joy experienced when the spirit becomes aware of itself is
like finally returning home after a long journey.
We find peace and security in the knowledge of our true essence
and are no longer fearful of death.

*

As we go through life,
our awareness never leaves us.
It is always present, even though
the specific thoughts and emotions
we experience may come and go.
See for yourself if it's possible to
run away from your awareness.

*

The awareness is akin to a vast, clear, and luminous blue sky.
Thoughts and emotions, like clouds, may appear temporarily,
but they cannot alter or tarnish the pristine nature of awareness.
Feel the immaculate quality of boundless silence in awareness.

*

Although the fish lives its life in the ocean,
it may not sense it because the ocean is too close.
Although the bird lives its life in the sky,
the bird may not know it because the sky is too vast.
Although we live in the field of limitless awareness,
we may miss it because the awareness is too transparent.

# The Tale of Roundy's Great Journey

There once was a cute little fish who lived in the middle of the Pacific Ocean. His head was rounder than the other fish's, so everyone called him "Roundy." Ever since he was young, Roundy had never been as interested in finding food or being as popular as other fish his age. His only interest was in meeting the great and holy being his grandfather had told him about, a being called "the Ocean." Grandfather, who raised Roundy, had told him that this Ocean had given life to all of creation, to everything that Roundy could see. He was kind and benevolent, creating enough nourishment for all living beings and accepting everyone equally without any discrimination. He would never boast about Himself or show His preference for one over another.

Roundy could only wonder in awe at how the Ocean could have the same love for ill-tempered Uncle Shark, who scared Roundy terribly, or ugly Auntie Lobster who had her sharp hands. Even though they might be unaware of Him, Grandfather said that the great Ocean was always near and knew every movement of all creation. So many of the fish, in difficult moments, would pray to the holy Ocean, and they developed the custom of offering Him precious pearls and valuable foods.

CURIOUSLY, THE NUMBER OF FISH who had actually seen the great Ocean with their own eyes or met Him in person was vanishingly small. There were only legends of a few special fish who, after a long journey in search of the Ocean, had barely managed to encounter Him. The journey they had undertaken required excruciating patience and effort, so most normal fish could not even conceive of going.

Roundy was told that the most difficult part was passing through the deep, dark Cave of Death, where even coral did not live; it was said that entering this cave, into which not even a single ray of light passed, was like experiencing death itself. So in order to pass through this cave you had to have faith in your heart, faith that the invisible Ocean was always at your side. But the time it took to pass through this cave was so long and terrifying that even fish with a strong faith and a tranquil mind would often give up halfway through or never make it back again.

So, when Roundy began preparing for the journey to meet the Ocean, his grandfather did not offer him words of encouragement; instead, he looked at him with a worried expression. He must have regretted ever telling Roundy about the Ocean.

Roundy's heart was heavy with worry as well, for he wondered who would take care of his grandfather if he should be hurt while passing through the Cave of Death or not return alive. But he could not give up. His desire to meet the great and holy Ocean was strong enough to overcome his worry and fear, and in the end, he convinced his grandfather and set out on his journey.

A MONTH AFTER HE HAD left home, Roundy finally arrived at the Cave of Death. He was excited and at the same time very scared. So, before entering the cave, Roundy offered up a heart-felt prayer: "Dear Benevolent Ocean, who is at my side, I want to meet you. Please guide me until I see you. I trust you." With that prayer, Roundy finally entered the cave, and the pitch-darkness enveloped him.

About half a day had passed since he had swum into the cave. In the midst of the perfect darkness, it was as if time stopped and his body disappeared. As time passed like a deep, dreamless sleep, the fear that had gripped him at first gradually faded away, to be replaced by a peaceful silence. Roundy was astonished that being unable to see or hear anything could be so peaceful and warm.

How many days had passed? A week or a month? All of a sudden, way off in the distance, Roundy saw a pinprick of light. As soon as he saw it, he instinctively began to swim toward it. A thought pierced the long silence and suddenly entered his mind: *Finally, I will leave the cave and meet the Ocean!* But in that very moment, a realization dawned on him. *What if this Ocean that I have been so eager to meet actually exists in the silence? Wasn't He present in the peaceful and comforting quiet of the cave as I passed through it? Just like my thought was born out of the silence, couldn't all other creations have arisen from the same silence?*

WHEN ROUNDY FINALLY CAME OUT of the cave, the sight that greeted his eyes was a familiar one of countless fish swimming peacefully in schools. But Roundy had begun to perceive not only the forms of those fish but also the transparent waters of the Ocean. He then said with a soft smile, "Now I can see you! I am in you! You are in me!" He finally realized that the journey to meet the great Ocean was not about finding a physical divine being, but about discovering His peaceful presence within himself. And from that day on, Roundy lived every moment with a deep sense of gratitude and connection to the Ocean, knowing that even in the darkest and most difficult times, the Ocean's presence and love would always be with him.

*

We shall not cease from exploration,
and the end of all our exploring will be
to arrive where we started
and know the place for the first time.
—T. S. Eliot

*

To those who are still reading:
May you be blessed with love and joy.
May you be surrounded by kindness and peace.
May you be guided by grace on your path.
May your life be filled with purpose and
meaningful experiences.